THE HOMERIC HYMNS

THE

HOMERIC HYMNS

Translation, Introduction, and Notes by
Apostolos N. Athanassakis

THIRD EDITION

Johns Hopkins University Press : Baltimore

© 1976, 2004, 2020 Johns Hopkins University Press
All rights reserved. Published 2020
Printed in the United States of America on acid-free paper
9 8 7 6 5 4 3 2 1

Johns Hopkins University Press
2715 North Charles Street
Baltimore, Maryland 21218-4363
www.press.jhu.edu

Library of Congress Cataloging-in-Publication Data

Names: Athanassakis, Apostolos N., translator, writer of supplementary
    textual content.
Title: The Homeric hymns / translation, introduction, and notes by
    Apostolos N. Athanassakis.
Other titles: Homeric hymns. English (Athanassakis)
Description: Third edition. | Baltimore : Johns Hopkins University Press,
    2020. | Includes bibliographical references and index.
Identifiers: LCCN 2019047582 | ISBN 9781421438603 (paperback) |
    ISBN 9781421438610 (ebook)
Subjects: LCSH: Homeric hymns—Translations into English. | Hymns,
    Greek (Classical)—Translations into English. | Gods, Greek—Poetry. |
    LCGFT: Poetry.
Classification: LCC PA4025.H8 A8 2020 | DDC 883/.01—dc23
LC record available at https://lccn.loc.gov/2019047582

A catalog record for this book is available from the British Library.

*Special discounts are available for bulk purchases of this book. For more
information, please contact Special Sales at specialsales@press.jhu.edu.*

Johns Hopkins University Press uses environmentally friendly book
materials, including recycled text paper that is composed of at least 30
percent post-consumer waste, whenever possible.

To my son, Nikolaos, and to my daughter, Yanoula

CONTENTS

PREFACE

MANY TRANSLATIONS of poetry are approximations of the original. However, every effort should be made to retain as much of the poetic beauty and impact of the original. In the present translation of the Homeric Hymns, I have aimed for accuracy at all times. Wherever I could, I tried to preserve for the reader the vigor and magic of the ancient text. In this third edition, I went somewhat further in modernizing traditional renditions of certain epithets and formulaic phrases. I also avoided lengthening or truncating lines so that the text would be more symmetrical. I made an effort to keep to an iambic flow without sacrificing accuracy.

The discussion of the authorship of the hymns is not productive anymore. Regardless of the status of the scholarly altercations at any given time, it is my sincere hope that the student of ancient Greek religion, mythology, and literature will not fail to see in the hymns a treasure trove of valuable information and charming poetry.

I have not succeeded in being consistent in the spelling of Greek names. I have made an effort, though, to follow the new trend that favors the Hellenic character of the names. In some cases, I allow the established Latinate or Anglicized form to remain. In the notes, I employ the macron sparingly to indicate vowel length and to avoid grossly infelicitous mispronunciation (e.g., Dymê, Dikê, Samê, to avoid confusion with "dime," "dike," "same," etc.).

References to ancient authors are usually from the *Oxford Classical Texts* (*OCT*). For the lyrical poets I have referred the reader to West (*Iambi et Elegi Graeci*, ed. M. L. West, Oxford, 1972), to the *PMG* (*Poetae Melici Graeci*, ed. Denys Page, Oxford, 1962), and to LP (*Poetarum Lesbiorum Fragmenta*, ed. Edgar Lobel and Denys Page, Oxford, 1955). Loeb, of course, refers to the three volumes of the *Lyra Graeca* subseries of the Loeb Classical Library, of which J. M. Edmonds is the translator. Bergk in parenthesis stands for Theodor Bergk's *Poetae Lyrici Graeci*. Because I cannot expect all readers to be familiar with abbreviations used by classicists, I should also clarify the following:

IG	*Inscriptiones Graecae*
CIG	*Corpus Inscriptionum Graecarum*
BCH	*Bulletin de Correspondence Hellénique*
Thuc.	Thucydides
Paus.	Pausanias
Arist.	Aristophanes

Throughout the preparation of the translation and the notes, I have had numerous occasions to make use of the learned commentary to the hymns by Allen, Halliday, and Sikes (1936).

The translation of the *Hymn to Demeter* inspired Susanna Coffey, now F.H. Sellers Professor at the School of the Art Institute of Chicago, to produce her own highly artistic opus (Kallichoron Press, 1988). Over the years, students in the College of Creative Studies at the University of California, Santa Barbara (UCSB), have written imaginative essays, mediated by previous editions. It would be an omission not to record here the fondest memories of teaching the Homeric Hymns to enthusiastic students in the very large classes on Greek mythology at UCSB.

Thanks to the continued support of Johns Hopkins University Press, the hymns have reached quite a large readership. I am grateful to the press for that.

My gratitude to Lloyd W. Daly and H.D.F. Kitto abides forever. Professor Daly taught me the hymns at the University of Pennsylvania. Kitto, as absolutely everyone called him at his own insistence, helped me come to the right word through parable and humorous anecdote. With regard to the second edition, two members of our staff, Anna Roberts and Liz Frech, deserve my appreciation for all manner of valuable assistance. Scott E. Rubin, one of our fine graduate students at that time, is to be thanked for his arduous bibliographical research. The genealogical charts benefited from the expert and much-appreciated touch of Timothy S. Heckenlively, a PhD in classics from UCSB and now senior lecturer in classics at Baylor University. Benjamin M. Wolkow, also a PhD in classics from UCSB and now a lecturer at the Department of Classics, University of Georgia, trued the final form of the entire text of the Homeric Hymns and worked most diligently on a thorough indexing of names and themes. To this end, Dr. Wolkow has contributed highly skilled labor as well as a rare combination of editorial and philological skill. All this contributed significantly to the integrity of the 2004 edition.

For the present third edition, I express my thanks to Angeliki Kourkouli, a graduate of the Agricultural University of Athens, for keeping track of details. Maria Legaki, a psychology graduate of the University of Kent, Canterbury, has become my devoted assistant. I thank her for her argus-eyed attention to matters of style. In this capacity, she scrutinized the entire text with meticulous care. I gladly acknowledge the loyal and competent assistance I have received from Konstantina Togka, who is on her last lap of receiving an MSc in nutrition and health studies at Wageningen University and Research of the Netherlands. Tim Vivian, now professor emeritus of religious studies at California State University, Bakersfield, has gone through the translation to remove any lingering stylistic infelicities.

INTRODUCTION

THE HOMERIC HYMNS have come down to us in a text that has been established quite securely through collation of thirty-one manuscripts that are scattered throughout various European libraries (the list can be found both in the *OCT* edition of the hymns and, in more detailed fashion, in the Allen, Halliday, and Sikes commentary, xi–xvii). That Greece should possess only one manuscript—the so-called *Athous* in the monastery of Vatopedi on Mt. Athos—is an indication both of the vicissitudes of Greek history and of the rapacity of conqueror and unscrupulous visitor. Of the existing thirty-one manuscripts, the best one is the *Mosquensis* (codex *M*). It is a late thirteenth- or early fourteenth-century manuscript that was discovered in the library of the Synod at Moscow in 1777. It now is in the possession of the University Library at Leiden. The hymns were included along with the *Iliad* and the *Odyssey* in the *editio princeps* of the Homerica, which was done in Florence by Demetrios Chalcocondyles in the year 1488. Both in antiquity and in modern times, the hymns have not been treated with the attention they deserve. For quite a long time in early antiquity they were attributed to Homer. Alexandrian scholars discarded the idea of Homeric authorship. Subsequently authorship always depended on literary fashion rather than verifiable fact.

From the fifth century we have a sole quotation of lines 3.146–50 and 3.165–72 of the *Hymn to Apollon* in Thucydides 3.104. The third-century scholar Antigonos of Karystos (fl. 240 BC) quotes one line from the *Hymn to Hermes* (4.51) in order to support the opinion that the guts of ewes, but not of rams, are "euphonic," that is, resonant enough to be used as lyre strings. To Diodorus Siculus (first century BC), we owe lines 1–9 of hymn 1 to Dionysos. Diodorus refers to the hymns three times in a manner that leaves it unclear whether he is quoting from the original (Diodorus Siculus 1.15.7; 3.66.3; 4.2.4). The only other first-century BC author to refer to the hymns is Philodemus in his *Peri Eusebeias*; the reference is to a word in line 2.440 of the *Hymn to Demeter*. In the second century AD, the references are equally scarce. Pausanias merely refers to the *Hymn to Demeter* twice (1.38.3; one of the references in this passage must be to a line not contained in the text as we now have it). He excerpts three lines (2.417, 418, 420) from the same hymn (4.30.3), and in a third reference calls upon the *Hymn to Apollon* to prove that Homer names the city below Delphoi, Krisa, in both the hymn as well as in the *Iliad* (2.520). Athenaeus is the first writer to use a quotation from the hymns (lines 3.514–16 from the *Hymn to Apollon*, found in Athenaeus 223) and to call into question

Homer's authorship. He implies that the *Hymn to Apollon* may have been written by one of the Homeridae, poets who followed Homer's style. From the same century, we have a quotation by the rhetor Aelius Aristides of lines 3.169–71 of the *Hymn to Apollon*.

Except for a few scattered references, chiefly by later scholiasts and antiquarians, the hymns seem to have suffered from a nearly universal literary conspiracy of silence. That we should have only scant evidence of their influence on classical authors is not so difficult to understand, but that the Alexandrian littérateurs and antiquarians should ignore this important body of literature we may benignly attribute to literary orthodoxy. It is interesting that no less a writer than Thucydides obviously accepted the tradition that ascribed the hymns to Homer, but the Alexandrian grammarians and critics made up their minds that the hymns had not been composed by the poet of the *Iliad* and the *Odyssey* and that, therefore, they did not deserve the attention lavished on Homer. There is no evidence that the Romans took notice of the hymns, and the Byzantines, obviously following the verdict of the Alexandrians, consigned them to the limbo of condescending indifference. In modern times, scholars have recognized the importance of the hymns, but students of the classics frequently bypass them for the study of the Homeric epics, and the educated public is hardly aware of their existence.

The tradition to which the Homeric Hymns belong may not be less pristine than that of the two great Homeric epics, which have so completely overshadowed them to the present day. Greek tradition has preserved the names of hymnists such as Orpheus, Linos, and Mousaios, who may have preceded Homer by hundreds of years. The term "hymnos" ("hymn") is generic and denotes a type of devotional song sung in honor of a god or a goddess, usually at a contest held as part of a religious festival or some other solemn occasion with religious overtones. The Homeric Hymns are distinguished from other hymnic poetry both by their meter—the dactylic hexameter—and by the formulae that the poet employs at the beginning and at the end of each poem. The ancients called these poems hymns, and specifically *prooimia* (preludes), because the poets used them as warm-up pieces for the singing or recitation of longer portions of the Homeric epics. Of the extant Homeric Hymns, four, to Demeter, Apollon, Hermes, and Aphrodite, are long enough to have been recited or sung independently. However, we cannot be sure that they too were not used as preludes to even more ambitious compositions. Not all the hymns seem equally devotional. The *Hymns to Hermes and Aphrodite*, for example, contain even comic elements, which, from our point of view, are hardly consonant with the spirit of piety that must permeate a religious occasion. Here, however, we must be careful not to project our own ideas of religious propriety onto those of the ancient Greeks, whose gods laughed and danced, whereas ours do not.

The *Hymn to Apollon* is the only one for which we have the name of the composer and what appears to be a false date. About the other hymns we do not know who composed them or when and where they were composed. Yet, internal evidence shows that some of them come from the eighth and seventh centuries, others from the sixth and fifth, and a very few are later, though not necessarily Hellenistic. We are therefore dealing with literary documents of great antiquity. Unfortunately, the ancients did not leave us learned commentaries on the hymns. Thus, we are tantalized by unexplained allusions and enigmatic statements. Even so, the hymns have much to tell us about Greek religion and mythology. There is no other single document, for example, that teaches us as much about Demeter and Apollon as the two long hymns to these gods. But a utilitarian view of the hymns is a very limited and unfair one. After all, we are dealing with poems and not with annalistic accounts. Two of the shorter hymns (7 and 19) and the four longer ones (2, 3, 4, and 5) are poems of great beauty and skill. Modern readers, who are not familiar with epic technique, may be taken aback by a pace that can be leisurely enough to digress exactly where we feel the action must go on and abruptly vigorous enough to begin totally *in medias res* (e.g., hymn 7). Surely, modern readers will weary of the list of places over which Apollon "ruled" (*Hymn to Apollon* 3.25–46), but they must be reminded that to the ancients it was important that due recognition be given to each of these places. Who can deny that poetic genius is at work in the *Hymn to Demeter* and in the incomparably subtle mixture of humor, seduction, and piety in the longer *Hymn to Aphrodite*? But the poets of the hymns do not need advocates or highly literate and fastidious readers. They need listeners who love good poetry for its own sake and who can believe that, if Jesus of Nazareth can resurrect the dead and turn water to wine, Apollon of Delphoi can change into a dolphin and, much like St. George, slay the dragon if he so wishes.

Professor Elroy Bundy in his long and learned essay "The Quarrel between Kallimachos and Apollonios" (*California Studies in Classical Antiquity* 5 [1972]: 39–94, and especially 49–55) has convincingly argued that the *khaire* of the rhapsodic *envoi* is more than just "hail" or "farewell." However, even if the meaning is more propitiatory than salutatory, the search for equivalents closer to the literal meaning—"be glad" or "rejoice"—is bound to be fruitless, as those who know the literal meaning of "good-bye" or "hail" will readily agree. It is only for lack of better approximations that I have retained the traditional translations. After all, *khaire* (now usually *khairete,* with allowances made for phonetic change of the sound *kh-*) may mean "hello" or "good-bye" in Greece today, but it may also mean "hail," as it does in the Greek national anthem. It all depends on the occasion and the context.

Recent years have witnessed a remarkable interest in the study of the hymns. Several new translations have made them accessible to the educated

public, as well as to thousands of students who study them chiefly as sources
for mythology in many colleges and universities across the United States and
even other countries. More scholars have turned their attention to the hymns
in innovative ways, and they have allowed such fields as anthropology, the
study of religion, and, in some cases, critical theory to enrich their understanding of this ancient poetry.

The Homeric Hymns are not all from the same age and not all of them
were composed for the same kind of religious occasion. The longer ones obviously come from times when oral poetry and religious beliefs were translated
into active participation in and observance of religious festivals, where long
hymns were valued and those who composed them were rewarded in concrete
and visible ways.

Annual feasts took place and they involved contests. The reader may wish
to pay special attention to 3.169–70, 6.19–21, and 26.12–13. A topic that deserves
close study, meticulous scrutiny, and also all the help that comparative anthropology can give us is the contribution of women to religious festivals and the
poetic contests that were an integral part of them. We must peer through the
multimillennial darkness to recapture, even in a sort of reverie, the rituals that
brought together the great goddess Demeter and the humble, down-to-earth
Iambe in the silent drama that followed Demeter's epiphany at the palace of
Keleos and Metaneira at Eleusis (2.184–209). Lines 3.156–76 of the *Hymn to
Apollon* (hymn 3 in the collection) pose a fascinating problem. We learn from
these lines that the Delian maidens played a central role in the festival honoring Apollon at Delos. They were "followers of the lord who shouts from afar."
They sang hymns. "The tongues of all men and their noisy chatter they know
how to mimic; such is their skill in composing songs that each man might
think he himself were speaking" (162–64). More important, a blind poet asks
them to choose him from among all other competing poets as their favorite.
Clearly, this poet was an oral poet. The Delian maidens may also have been
oral poets. Who were they? What did they do? What was the protocol for the
exceptional religious and poetic performance on the barren island of Delos?

It stands to reason that the shorter hymns are not the products of that
happy marriage between oral poetry and fervidly participatory religious piety.
It is no insult to the shorter hymns to suggest that later times, less religious
times that no longer honored the oral tradition, were content with a thrifty
and almost perfunctory poetic tribute to the gods.

We understand not a little about the Homeric Hymns. We are well
equipped to interpret certain aspects of them. Yet, charitably, we shall never
recapture the profound meaning of the poetic meadow in which Persephone
acts out the dreams of her innocence before she is carried away by Death—
Hades—the greatest rapist of them all.

Here are lines by which to live:

And they [the daughters of Keleos], as deer or calves in the season of
    spring
sated in their hearts with pasture frisk over a meadow,
held up the folds of their lovely robes
and darted along the hollow wagon-road, as their flowing hair
tossed about their shoulders, like the flowers of the crocus.

(*Hymn to Demeter*, 2.174–79)

Today, such young women may not be running to meet a goddess. They
may be jogging on campuses or in cities across the country. The beauty is
there, and it is timeless. The Homeric Hymns are songs of another time,
another place. To reach them requires transcending space and time. If we do
accomplish this impossible task, we may not only see but also feel the beauty
in the moment when a newborn god springs forth to the light, greeted by
screaming goddesses (3.119).

It should be pointed out that the hymns stay at a certain level of epic diction. There are very few details of real or everyday life. There are no spindles
and weavers. There is no plowing or threshing. Demeter is the great grieving
mother; a dark veil is a symbol of sorrow, but otherwise the poet doesn't say
much about what she wears. Likewise, Persephone is simply a beautiful young
maiden. The detail that Leto kneels on the grassy ground before she gives
birth to Apollon is a credible and down-to-earth one. Otherwise, it suffices
for the poet to present her as a Titaness. The divine baby obviously does not
need swaddling clothes. All this conforms to the norms of epic narrative. In
the *Iliad*, Andromache mourns the dead Hector. It is clear that she loved him
greatly. Yet no details are given. In the modern Greek folk songs, even when it
is clear that the talk is of lovers, nothing is said about details of intimacy. The
composers of the Homeric Hymns operated in the realm of the mythical past.
Details of everyday life and even of history were not relevant to them and to
their audiences. Sentiments were not included because those, too, were not
relevant to their stories. The only details mentioned were related to foun-
dational ritual. Thus, the *Hymn to Demeter* strengthens the claims of Eleusis
to the origin of the cult. Likewise, the story of Apollon's coming to Delphoi
strengthens the claims of Delphoi to the foundation of the cult of Apollon.
Important stations of life such as marriage and death are left out of the text. It
seems that even the social side of life was considered as belonging to another
genre of literature. We have no wedding in the hymns, but we do have the
details of Aphrodite's erotic epiphany to Anchises (5.53–175). One gets the
feeling that the text of the Homeric Hymns had to conform to certain norms,
which were not strictly religious. Quite a few of the hymns are too short to act
as warm-up pieces for major ones. So the question is, what was their function?

Is it possible that they served as mere reminders or that they were used for routine and very brief religious occasions?

An example for the idea suggested above is to be found in Orphic hymn 50 to Lysios Lenaios.

> A redeemer and a reveler you are,
> your thyrsus drives to frenzy,
> you are kind-hearted to all
> gods and mortals who see your light.
> I call upon you now,
> come, O sweet bringer of fruit.

In Homeric hymns 1 and 7, both devoted to Dionysos, there is not a hint of the spirit of these lines, of Dionysos as a reveler and redeemer. One wonders again what the particular religious inclination of the hymns was.

The occasions for performing the hymns may have originated from purely religious motives. In time such motives may have blended with social and commercial expedience. Delos offers an excellent example. It is no accident that the island became the seat of the Delian League.

Although the Homeric Hymns contain elements of prayer, there is no accumulation of epithets as in the Orphic Hymns. It may be that the Homeric Hymns contain no mystical element whatever. In Hesiod's *Theogony* we have the impressive lists of Nereids and Oceanines. With the exception of the list of the daughters of Okeanos, companions of Persephone (416–428), there are no such lists in the hymns.

The Greek language belongs to the great Indo-European (IE) family of languages. Homeric Greek is quite close to Vedic Sanskrit. It is also related to several other languages. It is quite close to Lithuanian and not so very far from the language of the Vikings, Old Norse. This kinship offers fascinating opportunities for study. Equally fascinating and challenging is the study of IE poetics. With a little bit of imagination, one will find similarities between some Vedic hymns and some of the hymns of the present collection. There are passages in Hesiod's *Works and Days* that remind one of the Icelandic Edda. In so many ways, such hymns as the one to Apollon and especially the one to Hermes in this collection are really poetic sagas. The complex question of the land of origin of the Indo-Europeans does not concern us here. It is quite probable that speakers of Greek invaded the Greek lands slowly when there were still nomadic or seminomadic tribes.

Zeus is clearly an Indo-European god. Thunder is his terrifying weapon. The Norse god Thor and his thunder offer a perfect analogy. The Aśvins of the Indic mythology correspond to the twin Dioskouroi of Greek mythology. Zeus is not the only god with an IE etymology. Ares, Poseidon, Hera, Eos, and quite likely Hermes have defensible IE origins. Functions of divinities merit careful study.

The IE social structure was tripartite. At the top of society were the priests, below them the warriors, and below the warriors the craftsmen. The goddess Athena represents this structure very clearly. She is the daughter of Zeus who very clearly—as shown by her helmet and spear—is a warrior goddess and also a protectress of craftsmen. The easiest, and sometimes the most interesting, IE words to track down are to be found in the spheres of kinship, parts, and fundamental functions of the human body.

Some of the hymns in the present collection are very short and have no plot. Such pieces may have been handy for musicians and comparable to very short prayers during the liturgy of the Christian church. The Homeric Hymns did not exist in a vacuum. Listeners must have connected them with art familiar to them from their religious practices. Visits to archaeological sites and museums can enhance understanding of these ancient texts. Also, epigraphic and numismatic evidence can be very helpful. It is very interesting that Athenian coins are, on the whole, limited to displaying the goddess Athena and her owl. Although the Eleusinian mysteries were so very important for the city of Athens, Demeter does not appear on the coins of Athens. Perhaps it was felt that the emblematic honor that came with the singular representation of Athena on coins of the city should not be shared with another divinity.

In the cosmology and mythic geography of very traditional Greek folk songs, heaven is nowhere to be found. In rare cases, we have references to the archangel Michael. In such cases the archangel escorts to heaven the souls of people who have died, while Charos (Hades) escorts souls from the Earth to the netherworld. Readers of the Homeric Hymns are urged to follow the results of excavations in various islands of the Aegean. In recent years, excavations at Keros, a very small island to the southeast of Naxos, and Despotiko, to the southwest of Antiparos, have brought to light a plethora of archaeological finds, as well as new information about settlements and holy places, especially in the area of Paros and Naxos.

I. Primeval Origins

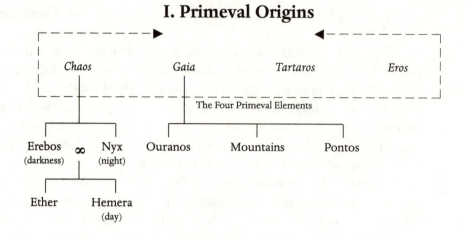

Chaos   *Gaia*   *Tartaros*   *Eros*

The Four Primeval Elements

Erebos (darkness) ∞ Nyx (night)   Ouranos   Mountains   Pontos

Ether   Hemera (day)

II. Genealogy of the Gods

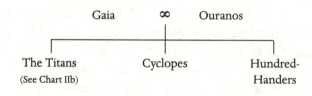

Gaia   ∞   Ouranos

The Titans (See Chart IIb)   Cyclopes   Hundred-Handers

IIb. The Titans and their Offspring

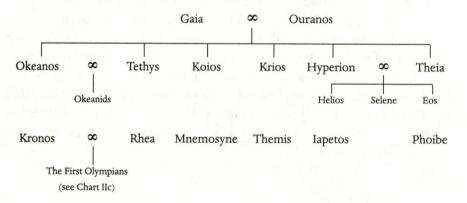

Gaia   ∞   Ouranos

Okeanos ∞ Tethys   Koios   Krios   Hyperion ∞ Theia

Okeanids   Helios   Selene   Eos

Kronos ∞ Rhea   Mnemosyne   Themis   Iapetos   Phoibe

The First Olympians (see Chart IIc)

Readers may wish to consult the index for more details.

IIc. The Olympian Gods*

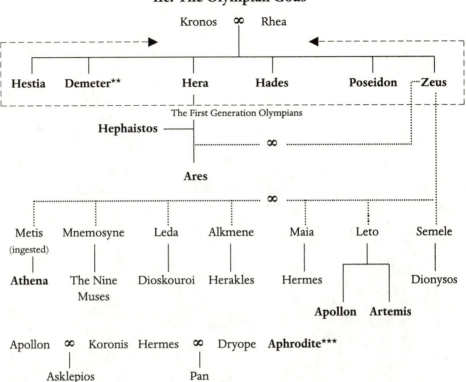

* Olympian gods are indicated in bold. The gods born of Kronos and Rhea are the older Olympians. The canon of the twelve Olympians came to include Athena, born of Zeus's own head; Hephaistos, the parthenogenetic son of Hera; and Hermes, son of Zeus and Maia. An incestuous union of Zeus and Hera produced Ares, while the Titaness Leto bore to Zeus Apollon and Artemis.

** Earth Mother of All (not to be confused with Gaia)—Rhea, Kybele, Mother of All, Mother of the Gods—shares a great deal with Demeter.

*** Aphrodite was born of the sea fecundated by the blood drops of the severed genitals of Ouranos.

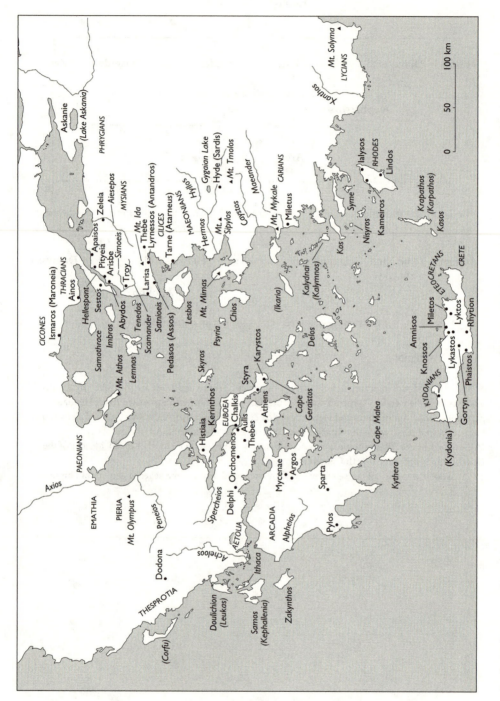

Preclassical Greece and Asia Minor. Drawn by William L. Nelson; adapted from J. D. Falconer and E. J. Owens in *Atlas of Classical History*, ed. R. J. A. Talbert, 9, 10 (London: Routledge, 1985).

THE HOMERIC HYMNS

1 : Fragments of the Hymn to Dionysos

(*Verses 1–9 are preserved by Diodorus Siculus 3.66.3*)
Some, O divine Eiraphiotes, say that you were born on Drakanon,
yet others claim it was on the wind-swept island of Ikaros, or even on Naxos,
and others that it was by the deep-eddying river Alpheios
that Semele conceived you and bore you to Zeus who delights in thunder.

5 And, O lord, some liars say you were born
at Thebes when in truth the father of gods and men
gave birth to you and hid you from the curiosity of mortals and of white-armed
    Hera.
There is a place called Nysa, a lofty mountain overgrown with trees,
far from Phoinike and near the flowing stream of Aigyptos.

(*Here begins folium 31 of codex* M):
10 "…And for her they will set up many statues in temples.
He cut you into three pieces, so in triennial feasts
men shall always sacrifice to you unblemished hecatombs."
So said Kronion and nodded with his dark brows,
and the lord's ambrosial mane streamed down

15 his immortal head and great Olympos shook.
So spoke Zeus the counselor and with a nod of his head he gave orders.
Eiraphiotes, woman-maddener, be propitious to us singers
who start and finish our song with you;
there is no way for the one who forgets you to remember his song.

20 So hail, Dionysos Eiraphiotes! Hail, Semele, his mother, called Thyône by others.

2 : To Demeter

I begin to sing of lovely-haired Demeter, the awesome goddess,
of her and her slender-ankled daughter whom Zeus,
far-seeing and loud-thundering, gave to Aidoneus to abduct.
Away from her mother of the golden sword and the splendid fruit

5 she played with the full-bosomed daughters of Okeanos,
gathering flowers, roses, crocuses, and beautiful violets
all over a soft meadow; irises, too, and hyacinths she picked,
and narcissus, which Gaia, pleasing the All-receiver,
made blossom there, by the will of Zeus, for a girl with a flower's beauty.

10 A lure it was, wondrous and radiant, and a marvel to be seen
by immortal gods and mortal men.
A hundred stems of sweet-smelling blossoms
grew from its roots. The wide sky above

and the whole earth and the briny swell of the sea laughed.
15 She was dazzled and reached out with both hands at once
to take the lovely delight; Earth with its wide roads gaped
and then over the Nysian field the lord and All-receiver,
the many-named son of Kronos, riding his immortal horses, sprang upon her.
Against her will he took her and on his golden chariot
20 carried her away. She wailed, and she raised a shrill cry,
calling upon father Kronides, the supreme Lord.
None of the immortals or of mortal men heard
her voice, not even the olive trees bearing splendid fruit.
Only the gentle-tempered daughter of Persaios,
25 Hekate of the shining headband, heard from her cave,
and lord Helios, the splendid son of Hyperion, also heard
the maiden calling on father Kronides; he sat
apart from the other gods, away in the temple of prayers,
as he received beautiful sacrifices from mortal men.
30 By Zeus's counsels, his brother, the All-receiver
and Ruler of Many, Kronos's son of the many names,
was carrying her away, against her will, on his chariot drawn by immortal horses.
So while the goddess looked upon the earth and the starry sky
and upon the swift-flowing sea teeming with fish
35 and the rays of the sun and still hoped to see
her loving mother and the races of gods immortal,
hope charmed her great mind, despite her grief.
The peaks of the mountains and the depths of the sea resounded
echoing her immortal voice, and her mighty mother heard her.
40 A sharp pain gripped her heart, and she tore
the headband round her divine hair with her own hands.
From both her shoulders she cast down her dark veil
and rushed like a bird over the nourishing land and over the sea,
searching; but none of the gods or mortal men
45 wanted to tell her the truth and none
of the birds of omen came to her as truthful messenger.
For nine days then all over the earth mighty Dêô
roamed about with bright torches in her hands,
and in her sorrow never tasted ambrosia
50 or nectar sweet to drink, and never bathed her body.
But when the tenth light-bringing Dawn came to her,
Hekate, carrying bright torches in her hands, met her,
and with loud voice spoke to her and told her the news:
"Mighty Demeter, bringer of seasons and of splendid gifts,
55 which of the heavenly gods or of mortal men

kidnapped Persephone and stabbed your dear heart with sorrow?
For I heard a voice but did not see with my own eyes
who it was. Here is a swift and accurate account."
So spoke Hekate, but the lovely-haired daughter of Rhea kept silent,
60   uttered not a single word, and both sped away
as Demeter held torches in her hands.
They came to Helios, spy on gods and men,
and they stood near his horses. The sublime goddess made out her case:
"Helios, do respect my divine status if I ever
65   cheered your heart and soul by word or deed.
Through the barren ether I heard the shrieking voice
of my daughter renowned for her beauty, a sweet flower at birth,
as if she were being overcome by force, but I saw nothing.
And since you do gaze down upon the whole earth
70   and sea and cast your rays through the bright ether,
tell me truly if you have seen anywhere
what god or even mortal man in my absence
kidnapped my dear child and then fled."
So she spoke and Hyperionidês replied to her:
75   "Lady Demeter, daughter of lovely-haired Rhea,
you shall know the truth; I greatly reverence and pity you
in your grief for your slender-ankled child; no other immortal
is to be blamed save cloud-gathering Zeus
who gave her to Hades, his own brother, to become
80   his buxom bride. He carried her away on his chariot,
down to misty darkness as she cried loud.
Goddess, cease your great wailing; you mustn't abandon
yourself to grief so overwhelming and fruitless. Not an unseemly
bridegroom among immortals is Aidoneus, lord of many,
85   your own true brother from the same seed; to his share fell
honor when in the beginning the triple division was made,
and he dwells among those over whom his lot made him lord."
With these words, he goaded his horses, and at his command
with the speed of long-winged birds, they drew the swift chariot,
90   as a pain more awful and more savage reached Demeter's heart.
Afterwards, angered with Kronion, lord of black clouds,
she withdrew from the assembly of the gods and from lofty Olympos
and wandered the cities of men and the wealth of their labors,
tearing at her fair form for a long time; no man
95   or deep-girded woman looking at her knew who she was
before she reached the house of prudent Keleos,
who then was lord of Eleusis, a town rich in sacrifices.

Grieving in her dear heart, she sat near the road,
at Parthenion, the well from which the citizens drew water,
100 as they sat under the shade of a bushy olive tree.
She looked like an old woman born a long time ago,
one no longer capable of childbearing and of enjoying the gifts of wreath-loving
   Aphrodite,
even as are nurses for the children of law-giving
kings and keepers of the storerooms in their bustling mansions.
105 The daughters of Keleos Eleusinides saw her
as they were coming to fetch easily-drawn water
in copper vessels to their father's own halls,
four of them in their maidenly bloom, like goddesses,
Kallidike, Kleisidike, and Demo the lovely,
110 and Kallithoe, who was the eldest of them all.
They did not know who she was; it is hard for mortals to see divinity.
They stood near her and spoke winged words:
"Aged lady, who are you? You are older, tell us of your generation.
Why have you wandered away from the city and not approached
115 our mansion? There in the shadowy halls live
women of your age and even younger ones
who will treat you kindly in both word and deed."
So they spoke, and the mighty goddess replied:
"Dear children, you obviously belong to nobility.
120 I greet you and I will explain; indeed it is fitting
to match your question with the truth,
Dôs is the name that my mighty mother gave me.
And now from Crete on the broad back of the sea
I came unwillingly; marauding men by brute force
125 carried me off against my will, and later
they landed their swift ship at Thorikos, where the women
came out in a body and the men themselves
prepared a meal by the stern cables of the ship.
But my heart had no desire for the evening's sweet meal;
130 I eluded them and, rushing through the dark land,
I fled my reckless masters, so that they might not enjoy
the price set on my head, since, like pirates they carried me across the sea.
So I have wandered to this place and know not at all
what kind of land this is and what sort of men live in it.
135 But may all who dwell in the Olympian halls
grant you men to wed and bear children
as your parents wish. And now have pity on me, maidens,
and, dear children, kindly let me seek shelter at someone's house,

where there is a head of the house, man or woman, to do chores for them
140   in such tasks as befit a woman past her prime.
I shall hold the newborn child in my arms.
I shall take care of the house,
I will surely make my master's bed in the deep recess of the house,
in the elegant bedroom, and I shall keep a watchful eye on the duties of his
     ladywife."
145   So spoke the goddess, and soon Kallidike, still an untouched virgin,
and the most beautiful of Keleos's daughters, replied:
"Auntie, men must take the gifts of the gods
even when they bring them pain, since gods are truly much stronger.
I shall give you a clear account, indeed I shall give you the names
150   of the men who have great power and honor in this place;
here are the names of the people who defend the towers
of the city by their counsels and straight judgments.
They are Triptolemos, shrewd in counsel, and Dioklos,
Polyxeinos, and Eumolpos, untainted by blame,
155   Dolichos and our lordly father.
Everyone has a wife who manages his mansion.
No woman there, when she first looks upon you,
will dishonor your appearance and remove you from the mansion,
but each will receive you, for indeed you look like a goddess.
160   If you wish, please wait here for us to go to the mansion
of our father and tell our deep-girded mother, Metaneira,
all these things from beginning to end, hoping that
she will ask you to come to our mansion and not search for another host.
A growing son is being raised in the well-built mansion
165   born late in her life, much prayed for and welcome.
If you should bring him up to reach puberty,
some tender-hearted woman might easily envy you,
upon laying eyes on you; such rewards for rearing him our mother will give you."
So she spoke, and the goddess nodded her head in assent.
170   They proudly carried their shining vessels filled with water.
Swiftly they reached their father's great mansion and quickly told
their mother what they had seen and heard. She commanded them
to go at once and invite the lady to come for generous wages.
And they, as deer or calves in the season of spring
175   sated in their hearts with pasture frisk over a meadow,
held up the folds of their lovely robes
and darted along the hollow wagon-road, as their flowing hair
tossed about their shoulders, like the flowers of the crocus.
They met the glorious goddess near the road where

180   they had left her before; and then they led her to their father's
         house. The goddess walked behind them, brooding
         in her heart, with her head covered, while a dark
         cloak swirled about her soft feet.
         Soon they reached the house of Zeus-cherished Keleos
185   and through the portico they went where their lady mother
         sat by a pillar, which supported the close-fitted roof,
         holding tight to her breast a child, a young blossom. They ran near her,
         and the goddess stepped on the threshold and touched
         the roof beam with her head and filled the doorway with divine radiance.
190   Awe, reverence, and pale fear seized the mother;
         and she yielded her seat to the goddess and asked her to sit.
         But Demeter, the bringer of seasons and splendid gifts,
         did not want to sit on the lustrous, luxurious seat;
         she kept silent and cast down her beautiful eyes
195   until Iambê, ever so aware of her duties, placed in front of her
         a well-fitted seat and over it threw a white fleece.
         Demeter sat on it and held her veil in front of her,
         remaining long on the seat, speechless and brooding,
         doing nothing and speaking to nobody.
200   Without laughing or tasting food or drink
         she sat pining with longing for her deep-girded daughter
         until Iambê, ever so aware of her duties, with her jokes
         and many jests moved the pure and mighty one
         to smile and laugh and have a gracious temper.
205   At later times, too, Iambê was able to please her moods.
         Metaneira now filled a cup with wine and gave it
         to her, but she refused it; it was not right for her, she said,
         to drink red wine. She asked them to give her a drink
         of barley-meal and water mixed with tender pennyroyal.
210   Metaneira mixed the drink and gave it to the goddess, as she had asked,
         and mighty Dêô accepted it, complying with holy custom.
         Then among them fair-girded Metaneira started speaking.
         "I salute you, lady, because I think you were born to noble
         and not to lowly parents. Modesty and grace show
215   in your eyes, as if you were the child of lawgiving kings.
         But men must take the gifts of the gods even when they are
         grieved by them, for on their necks there is a yoke.
         You are here now, our guest, and what is mine will be yours.
         Nurture this child of mine, unexpected and late-born,
220   a gift of the gods, in answer to my many prayers.
         If you should bring him up to reach the age of puberty,

some tender-hearted woman may look upon you with envy;
such rewards for rearing him I will give you."
Fair-wreathed Demeter took her turn and spoke to her:

225 "I salute you too, lady; may the gods grant you good things.
I will gladly accept the child as you ask me.
I will nurture him and I don't think that for his nurse's foolishness
either a spell or the Undercutter will harm him.
I know a remedy by far mightier than the tree-felling creature,

230 and for harmful bewitching I know a noble antidote."
With these words she received him to her fragrant bosom
and to her immortal arms, and the mother rejoiced in her heart.
Thus the fine son of prudent Keleos,
Demophoön, to whom fair-girded Metaneira gave birth,

235 was nurtured by her in the palace, and grew up to be like a god,
not eating food nor nursing at his mother's breast.
As if he were the child of a god, Demeter anointed him with ambrosia,
holding him to her bosom and breathing on him sweetly.
At night she hid him in the blazing fire like a firebrand,

240 secretly from his loving parents. To them it was a miracle
how he blossomed forth and looked like the gods.
She would have made him ageless and immortal,
if fair-girded Metaneira, thinking foolish thoughts
and keeping watch by night from her sweet-smelling chamber,

245 had not seen her; she raised a cry, then struck her thighs
in fear for her child, and blindness entered her mind.
She wept and spoke winged words:
"Demophoön, my child, this stranger hides you
in a great fire, bringing me grief and painful care."

250 So she spoke, wailing, and the splendid goddess heard her.
Shafts of terrible anger shot through Demeter,
the fair-wreathed, who then with her immortal hands
took from the blazing fire and placed on the ground
the dear child born in the queen's mansion,

255 and at the same time spoke to fair-girded Metaneira:
"Mortals are too foolish to know ahead of time
the measure of good and evil that is yet to come.
You, too, were greatly blinded by your foolishness.
The relentless water of the Styx by which gods swear

260 be my witness. I would have made your dear son
ageless and immortal, honored forever,
but now he cannot escape the fate of death.
Yet, honor everlasting shall be his because

he climbed on my knees and slept in my arms.
265   In due time and as the years revolve for him,
the sons of the Eleusinians will join in war
and dreadful battle against each other forever.
I am Demeter the honored, the greatest
benefit and joy to undying gods and to mortals.
270   But come now, let all the people build me
a great temple and beneath it an altar under the steep walls
of the city, above Kallichoron, on the rising hill.
I myself shall introduce rites so that later
you may propitiate my mind by their proper performance."
275   With these words the goddess changed her size and form
and sloughed off old age, as beauty was wafted all about her.
From her fragrant veils a lovely smell
emanated, and from the immortal body of the goddess light
shone afar, as her blond hair streamed down over her shoulders,
280   and the sturdy mansion was filled with radiance as if from lightning.
Out she went through the mansion. The queen staggered,
and she remained speechless for a long time, forgetting
to pick up her growing child from the floor.
His sisters heard his pitiful voice,
285   and they ran from their beds, so beautifully covered; then one
took up the child in her arms and held him to her bosom.
Another revived the fire and yet a third rushed
on her tender feet to rouse her mother from her sweet-smelling chamber.
They gathered round the squirming child, bathed him,
290   and fondled him, but his heart was not soothed,
for surely lesser nurses and governesses held him now.
All night long they propitiated the glorious goddess,
quaking with fear, and as soon as dawn appeared
they told the truth to Keleos, whose power reached far,
295   as the fair-wreathed goddess Demeter had ordered them.
He then called to assembly the people of every district
and ordered them to build a lavish temple to lovely-haired Demeter
and make an altar on the rising hill.
They listened to his speech, obeyed it in haste, and built
300   the temple according to divine decree and royal order.
Now when they finished the temple and refrained from labor,
each man went to his home, but blond Demeter,
sitting there apart from all the blessed ones,
kept on wasting with longing for her wasp-waisted daughter.
305   Onto the much-nourishing earth she brought a year

most dreadful and harsh for men; no seed
in the earth sprouted, for fair-wreathed Demeter concealed it.
In vain the oxen drew many curved plows over the fields,
and in vain did much white barley fall into the furrows.
310 She would have destroyed the whole race of mortal men
with painful famine and would have deprived
the Olympians of the glorious honor of gifts and sacrifices,
if Zeus had not perceived this and pondered it in his mind.
First he sent gold-winged Iris to invite
315 lovely-haired and beautiful Demeter to come.
He spoke to her and she obeyed Zeus, the son of Kronos and lord
of dark clouds, and ran swiftly midway between earth and sky.
She reached the town of Eleusis rich in sacrifices,
found the dark-veiled Demeter in the temple
320 and to her she spoke, winged words:
"Demeter, Zeus the father, whose wisdom never wanes,
invites you to come among the tribes of the immortal gods.
But come and let not the word of Zeus be unaccomplished."
So she spoke, begging her, but she could not bend the mind of the goddess.
325 So then again the father sent forth all the blessed
immortal gods. They ran to her, and each in his turn
summoned her and gave her many beautiful gifts
and whatever honors she might want to choose among the immortals.
But no one could persuade the mind and thought
330 of the angry goddess who stubbornly spurned their offers.
She said she would never set foot on fragrant Olympos
and never allow the grain in the earth to sprout forth
before seeing with her eyes her daughter's lovely face.
So when loud-thundering, far-seeing Zeus heard this,
335 he sent Argeiphontes of the golden wand to Erebos.
His mission was to win Hades over with gentle words,
and bring Persephone out of misty darkness
to light and among the gods, so that her mother
might see her with her own eyes and cease her anger.
340 Hermes did not disobey and, leaving his Olympian seat,
with eager speed he plunged down toward the earth.
He found the lord of the underworld inside his dwelling,
sitting on his bed with his revered spouse; Persephone was
in many ways reluctant and missed her mother, who now
345 had a plan apart from the blessed gods and their deeds.
Mighty Argeiphontes stood near and spoke to him:
"Hades, dark-haired lord of those who have perished,

Zeus the father bids you bring noble Persephone
out of Erebos and among the gods, so that her mother
350   may see her with her own eyes and cease her anger
and dreadful wrath against the gods; she is plotting
utter devastation against the feeble races of earth-born men.
The seed will be hidden under the earth and the immortals will lose
their honors. Her anger is relentless, and she does not mingle
355   with the gods, but apart from them in her fragrant temple
she sits, dwelling in the rocky town of Eleusis."
Thus he spoke and Aidoneus, lord of the netherworld,
with smiling brows obeyed the behests of Zeus the king
and speedily gave his command to prudent-minded Persephone:
360   "Persephone, go to your dark-robed mother,
with a gentle spirit and temper in your breast,
and in no way be more dispirited than the other gods.
I shall not be an unfitting husband among the immortals,
as I am father Zeus's own brother. When you are here
365   you shall be mistress of everything that lives and moves;
your honors among the immortals shall be the greatest,
and those who wrong you shall always be punished,
if they do not appease your spirit with sacrifices,
performing sacred rites and making due offerings."
370   So he spoke and wise Persephone rejoiced
and swiftly sprang up for joy, but he himself
gave her to eat a honey-sweet pomegranate seed,
contriving secretly about her, so that she might not spend
all her days again with dark-robed, revered Demeter.
375   Aidoneus, ruler of many, harnessed the immortal horses nearby
to the golden chariot.
She mounted the chariot, and next to her mighty Argeiphontes
took the reins and the whip in his own hands
and sped out of the halls, as the horses flew readily.
380   Soon they reached the end of the long path, and neither
the sea nor the water of rivers nor the grassy glens
and mountain-peaks checked the onrush of the immortal horses,
but they went over all these, traversing the lofty air.
He drove them and then halted near the fragrant temple
385   where fair-wreathed Demeter stayed. When she saw them,
she rushed like a maenad in a shady woodland on the mountains.
Persephone on her part, when she saw the beautiful eyes
of her mother, leaving chariot and horses, leaped down
to run and to throw her arms round her mother's neck.

390 And as Demeter still held her dear child in her arms,
   her mind suspected trickery, and in awful fear she withdrew
   from fondling her and at once asked her a question:
   "Child, when you were below, did you perhaps partake
   of food? Speak out, that we both may know.
395 If your answer is no, coming up from loathsome Hades,
   you shall dwell both with me and with father Kronion,
   lord of dark clouds, honored by all the immortals.
   Otherwise, you shall fly and go to the depths of the earth
   to dwell there a third of the seasons in the year,
400 spending two seasons with me and the other immortals.
   Whenever the earth blooms with every kind of sweet-smelling
   springflower, you shall come up again from misty darkness,
   a great wonder for gods and mortal men.
   With what trick did the mighty All-receiver deceive you?"
405 Facing her now, beautiful Persephone replied:
   "Surely, Mother, I shall tell you the whole truth.
   When Hermes, the helpful swift messenger, came
   from father Zeus and the other sky-dwellers
   to fetch me from Erebos, so that seeing me with your own eyes
410 you might cease your anger and dreadful wrath against the immortals,
   I myself sprang up for joy, but Aidoneus slyly placed
   in my hands a pomegranate seed, sweet as honey to eat, and
   against my will and by force he made me taste of it.
   How he abducted me through the shrewd scheming of Kronides,
415 my father, and rode away carrying me to the depths of the earth
   I shall explain and rehearse every point as you are asking.
   All of us maidens in a delightful meadow,
   Leukippe, Phaino, Electra, Ianthe,
   Melite, Iache, Rhodeia, Kallirhoe,
420 Melobosis, Tyche, Okyrhoe with a face like a flower,
   Chryseis, Ianeira, Akaste, Admete,
   Rhodope, Plouto, lovely Kalypso,
   Styx, Ourania, charming Galaxaura,
   battle-stirring Pallas, and arrow-pouring Artemis,
425 were playing and picking lovely flowers with our hands,
   mingling soft crocuses and irises with hyacinths
   and the flowers of the rose and lilies, a wonder to the eye,
   and the narcissus, which the wide earth grows crocus-colored.
   So I myself was picking them with joy, but the earth beneath
430 gave way and from it the mighty lord and All-receiver
   leapt out. He carried me under the earth in his golden chariot,

though I resisted and shouted with shrill voice.
I am telling you the whole truth, even though it grieves me."
So then all day long, being one in spirit,
435 they warmed each other's hearts and minds in many ways
with loving embraces, and an end to sorrow came to their hearts,
as they took joys from each other and gave in return.
Hekate of the shining headband came near them
and many times lovingly touched the daughter of pure Demeter.
440 From then on this lady became Persephone's attendant and follower.
Far-seeing, loud-thundering Zeus sent them a messenger,
lovely-haired Rhea, to bring her dark-veiled mother
among the races of the gods, promising to give her
whatever honors she might choose among the immortal gods.
445 With a nod of his head he promised that, as the year revolved,
her daughter could spend one portion of it in the misty darkness
and the other two with her mother and the other immortals.
He spoke and the goddess did not disobey the behests of Zeus.
Speedily she rushed down from the peaks of Olympos
450 and came to Rharion, life-giving udder of the earth
in the past, and then no longer life-giving but lying idle
without a leaf. It was now hiding the white barley
according to the plan of fair-ankled Demeter, but later
the fields would be plumed with long ears of grain,
455 as the spring waxed, and the rich furrows on the ground
teemed with ears to be bound into sheaves by withes.
There she first landed from the unharvested ether.
Joyfully they beheld each other and rejoiced in their hearts;
and Rhea of the shining headband spoke to her:
460 "Come, child! Far-seeing, loud-thundering Zeus invites you
to come among the races of the gods and promises to give you
whatever honors you wish among the immortal gods.
With a nod of his head he said that this promise would be brought to pass,
your daughter could spend one portion of the year in the misty darkness
465 and the other two with you and the other immortals.
With a nod of his head he said it would thus be brought to pass.
But obey me, my child! Come and do not nurse
unrelenting anger against Kronion, lord of dark clouds;
soon make the life-giving seed grow for men."
470 So she spoke and fair-wreathed Demeter did not disobey,
but swiftly made the seed sprout out of the fertile fields.
The whole broad earth teemed with leaves and flowers;
and she went to the kings who administer the laws,

Triptolemos and Diokles, smiter of horses, and mighty Eumolpos
475   and Keleos, leader of the people, and showed them
the celebration of holy rites, and explained to all,
to Triptolemos, to Polyxeinos, and also to Diokles,
that the awesome mysteries should not be transgressed, violated,
or divulged, because the tongue is restrained by reverence for the gods.
480   Blessed on this earth is the one who has seen these rituals
but the one who has no part in the holy rites has
another lot as he wastes away in dank darkness.
After splendid Demeter had counseled the kings in everything,
she and her daughter went to Olympos to be with the other gods.
485   There they dwell beside Zeus who delights in thunder,
commanding awe and reverence; thrice blessed is he
of men on this earth whom they gladly favor.
Soon to his great house they send as guest
Ploutos, who brings wealth to mortal men.
490   But come now, you who dwell in the fragrant town of Eleusis,
sea-girt Paros and rocky Antron,
mighty mistress Dêô, bringer of seasons and splendid gifts,
both you and your daughter, lovely Persephone,
for my song kindly grant me possessions pleasing the heart,
495   and I shall remember you and another song as well.

3 : To Apollon

Memory must now turn to Far-shooting Apollon.
The gods of the house of Zeus tremble at his coming,
and at once all spring up from their seats
as he approaches, stringing his splendid bow.
5   Leto alone remains by Zeus who delights in thunder
to unstring Apollon's bow and close his quiver;
from his mighty shoulders with her hands she takes
the bow and hangs it from a golden peg on her father's own post,
and after that she leads him to a seat.
10   Then his father offers him nectar in a golden goblet
and drinks a toast to his beloved son;
the other gods sit down as mighty Leto rejoices,
because she gave birth to a mighty son, an archer.
Hail, O blessed Leto, because you gave birth to illustrious children,
15   lord Apollon and arrow-pouring Artemis,
to her on Ortygia and to him on rocky Delos,
as you leaned against the towering mass of the Kynthian hill,

very near a palm tree by the stream of the Inopos.
How shall I match the hymns already sung in your honor?

20   For everywhere, Phoibos, singing is in your domain,
both on the islands and on the mainland, which abounds with herds of calves.
All peaks and high ridges of lofty mountains
and rivers flowing seawards and harbors of the sea
and beaches sloping toward it give you pleasure.

25   Shall I sing how first Leto gave birth to you, a joy to mortals,
as she leaned against Mount Kynthos, on the rocky and sea-girt
island of Delos, while on either side a dark wave
swept landwards driven by shrill winds?
From there you arose to rule over all mortal men:

30   over the inhabitants of Crete and of the city of Athens,
of Aigina and Euboea, famous for ships,
of Aigai and Eiresiai and Peparêthos by the sea,
of Thracian Athos and Pelion's towering peaks,
of Thracian Samos and Ida's shady mountains,

35   of Skyros and Phôkaia and Autokanê's steep heights,
of well-built Imbros and Lêmnos, enveloped in haze,
of holy Lesbos, realm of Makar, son of Aiolos,
of Chios, brightest of all the islands lying in the sea,
of craggy Mimas and the lofty peaks of Kôrykos,

40   of shimmering Klaros and Aisageê's dizzying heights,
of well-watered Samos and Mykalê's towering peaks,
of Miletos and Kos, city of Meropian men,
of rugged Knidos and wind-swept Karpathos,
of Naxos and Paros and rocky Rhênaia.

45   So many places did Leto visit, in travail with the Far-shooter,
searching for a land that would give him a home.
But they trembled greatly in fear, and none dared—
not even the richer ones—to be a host to Phoibos,
until indeed mighty Leto set foot on Delos

50   and made an inquiry, speaking winged words to her:
"Delos, would you want to be the abode of my son,
Phoibos Apollon, and to house him in a lavish temple?
For it cannot escape you that no other will touch you
since I think you shall never be rich in oxen or sheep

55   and shall never produce vintage nor grow an abundance of plants.
If you have a temple for Apollon who shoots from afar,
then all men shall gather here and bring
hecatombs, and the ineffably rich savor of burning fat
shall always rise, and you shall feed your dwellers

60   from the hands of strangers, since your soil is barren."
      So she spoke. Then Delos rejoiced and replied:
      "Leto, most glorious daughter of great Koios,
      I would gladly receive your offspring, the lord
      who shoots from afar; since truly the sound of my name
65   is hideous to men, thereby I would be greatly honored.
      But, Leto, I shall not hide the fear this word brings me.
      They say that Apollon will be haughty
      and greatly lord it over the immortal gods
      and the mortal men of the barley-bearing earth.
70   So I dreadfully fear in my heart and soul
      that, when he first sees the light of the sun, he might
      scorn an island whose ground is rocky, and that
      he might overturn me with his feet and push me into the deep sea.
      A great billow will always flood me
75   up to my highest peak, while he arrives at another land,
      where it may please him to establish a temple surrounded by wooded groves.
      Then polyps will settle on me and black seals on me
      will make their carefree abodes where there are no people.
      But, goddess, if only you would deign to swear a great oath,
80   that here first he would build a beautiful temple
      to be an oracle for men and afterwards

      .   .   .   .

      among all men, since today many are his names."
      So she spoke, and Leto swore the great oath of the gods:
      "Earth be my witness and the wide sky above
85   and the cascading water of the Styx, which is the greatest
      and most awful oath among the blessed gods,
      that here there shall always be a fragrant altar and a temple
      for Phoibos and that he shall honor you above all others."
      When she swore and completed her oath
90   the Far-shooting lord's expected birth brought great joy to Delos;
      for nine days and nine nights Leto was racked
      by unexpected travail. The goddesses were all with her—
      the best ones, that is—such as Dione, Rhea,
      Ichnaian Themis, loud-groaning Amphitrite,
95   and other immortal goddesses save white-armed Hera,
      who sat in the palace of cloud-gathering Zeus.
      Only Eileithyia, goddess of labor pains, did not find out,
      for she sat on top of Olympos under golden clouds,
      through the counsels of white-armed Hera, who restrained her
100   out of jealousy, because fair-tressed Leto

was about to give birth to a mighty and blameless son.
They sent Iris forth from the well-built island
to bring Eileithyia, promising a great necklace
nine cubits long and held together by golden threads.

105   And they bid Iris call her apart from white-armed Hera fearing that
she might persuade Eileithyia not to go.
When swift Iris, fleet of foot as the wind, heard this,
she set out to run and quickly traversed all the midspace.
When she reached lofty Olympos, the seat of the gods,

110   at once she called Eileithyia out of the palace
to the doors, spoke to her with winged words and
told her all, as she had been commanded by the Olympian goddesses.
She did persuade her heart in her dear breast
and as they went their gait was like that of timid doves.

115   When Eileithyia, goddess of travail, set foot on Delos,
the pains of labor seized Leto, and she yearned to give birth.
She threw her two arms round a palm tree, and propped her knees
on the soft meadow while the earth beneath her was all smiles.
Apollon lunged at the light, and all the goddesses screamed.

120   Then, noble Phoibos, the goddesses bathed you pure and clean
with fresh water and swaddled you in a white sheet,
fine and new-woven, and around you they wrapped a golden band.
Nor did his mother nurse Apollon of the golden sword
but Themis poured for him nectar and lovely ambrosia

125   with her immortal hands, and Leto rejoiced
for giving birth to a mighty son, a great archer.
But when, O Phoibos, you devoured this food for immortals,
neither golden bands could hold you as you struggled
nor bonds restrain you, for their ends came loose.

130   Soon among the goddesses spoke Phoibos Apollon:
"My wish is to hold dear the lyre and the curved bow
and to reveal to men the unerring will of Zeus."
With these words the long-haired, Far-shooting god
walked away over the earth and its wide roads, and all

135   the goddesses were dazzled while all of Delos,
now laden with gold, looked upon the offspring of Zeus and Leto,
and rejoiced, because from among the islands and the mainland
a god chose her to be his dwelling and loved her dearly in his heart;
she bloomed like a mountain peak overgrown with the flowers of the forest.

140   You yourself, Far-shooting lord of the silver bow,
sometimes set foot on rocky Kynthos
while at other times you roam among islands and among men.

Many temples and wooded groves are yours,
and all the peaks and towering crags of lofty mountains
145 and rivers flowing forth to the sea are dear to you.
But it is in Delos, O Phoibos, that your heart delights the most,
for Ionians in trailing garments gather there
in your honor together with their children and modest wives.
With boxing matches, dancing, and song,
150 they delight you and remember you whenever they hold their contests.
Whoever comes upon the Ionians, when they are gathered,
might think they were forever immortal and ageless.
For he would see their grace and delight his soul,
looking upon the fair-girded women and the men
155 with their swift ships and their many possessions.
There is also a great wonder of everlasting renown,
the Delian maidens, followers of the lord who shoots from afar.
After they first praise Apollon with a hymn
and now again Leto and arrow-pouring Artemis,
160 they tell of men and women who lived long ago
and sing a hymn, charming the races of men.
The tongues of all men and their noisy chatter
they know how to mimic; such is their skill in composing song
that each man might think he himself were speaking.
165 But now may Apollon and Artemis be propitious;
all you maidens, farewell. I ask you to call me to mind
in time to come whenever some man on this earth,
a stranger whose suffering never ends, comes here and asks:
"Maidens, which of the singers, a man wont to come here,
170 is to you the sweetest, and in whom do you most delight?"
Do tell him in unison that I am he,
a blind man, dwelling on the rocky island of Chios,
whose songs shall all be the best in time to come.
I will carry your renown as far as I roam
175 over the lands of men and their cities of fair locations.
Indeed they will not doubt this because it is true.
I shall not cease to hymn Far-shooting Apollon,
lord of the silver bow and child of lovely-haired Leto.
O lord, yours is Lykia and Meonia the lovely
180 and Miletos, too, the enchanting city by the sea,
and you again greatly rule over wave-washed Delos.
The son of glorious Leto goes to rocky Pytho,
playing his hollow lyre,
and wearing garments divine and fragrant; his lyre

185 struck by the golden plectrum gives an enchanting sound.
     From there, fleet as thought, he leaves the earth for Olympos
     and goes to the palace of Zeus and the company of the other gods.
     Swiftly the immortals take interest in his song and lyre,
     and all the Muses, answering with beautiful voices,
190 hymn the divine gifts of the gods and the hardships
     brought upon men by the immortal gods.
     Men live an unresourceful and thoughtless life, unable
     to find a cure for death and a charm to repel old age.
     The fair-tressed Graces and the kindly Seasons
195 and Harmonia and Hebe and Aphrodite, the daughter of Zeus,
     dance, each holding the other's wrist.
     Among them sings one, neither ugly nor slight of stature
     but truly of great size and marvelous aspect,
     arrow-pouring Artemis, Apollon's twin sister.
200 With them play Ares and keen-eyed Argeiphontes;
     Phoibos Apollon, his step high and stately, plays the lyre,
     enveloped in the brilliance of his glittering feet
     and well-woven garment.
     Leto of the golden tresses and Zeus the counselor
205 rejoice in their great souls as they look upon
     their beloved son playing music among the immortals.
     How shall I match the hymns already sung in your honor?
     Am I to sing of you as suitor and lover of maidens,
     sing how, courting the daughter of Azas, you raced
210 against godlike Ischys Elationides, owner of fine horses,
     or against Phorbas sprung from Triops or against Ereutheus?
     Or in the company of Leukippos and his wife,
     you on foot and he on horseback? He surely was as good as Triops!
     Or am I to sing how at first you went all over the earth,
215 seeking the seat of an oracle, O Far-shooting Apollon?
     To Pieria you first descended from Olympos
     and made your way past sandy Lektos and the Ainianes
     and Perrhaiboi; and soon you reached Iolkos
     and set foot on Kenaion in Euboea, renowned for ships;
220 you stood on the Lelantine plain, but it did not please
     your heart to build a temple surrounded by wooded groves there.
     Next, O Far-shooting Apollon, you crossed Euripos
     and went along a sacred green mountain, and then you left
     to come to Mykalessos and grassy-bedded Teumessos.
225 Soon you arrived at the forest-covered abode of Thebe;
     no mortal as yet lived in sacred Thebe,

and at that time there were no paths or roads yet
throughout the wheat-bearing plain of Thebe, but forests covered it.
From there, O splendid Apollon, you went onward
230   to reach Onchestos, the fair grove of Poseidon,
where a new-broken colt, vexed as he is at drawing
the beautiful chariot, slows down to breathe, as its noble driver
leaps down from the chariot and goes his way; and the horses
for some time rattle the empty chariot, free from their master's control.
235   If they should break the chariot in the wooded grove,
the horses are taken away but the tilted chariot is left behind.
For such is the ancient custom: they pray to the lord
while to the god's lot falls the custody of the chariot.
You soon left that place, O Far-shooting Apollon,
240   and then reached the beautiful streams of Kephissos,
which pours forth its fair-flowing water from Lilaia.
And, O long distance archer, you crossed it and many-towered Okalea,
and from there you arrived at grassy Haliartos.
You set foot on Telphousa, where the peaceful place
245   pleased you, and so you built a temple surrounded by wooded groves.
Standing very close to her you spoke these words:
"Telphousa, here I intend to build a beautiful temple
to be an oracle for men who will always
bring to me here unblemished hecatombs;
250   and as many as dwell on fertile Peloponnesos
and on Europe and throughout the sea-girt islands
will consult it. It is my wish to give them unerring
advice, making prophecies inside the lavish temple."
With these words Phoibos Apollon laid out the foundations,
255   broad and very long from beginning to end; Telphousa saw this
and with anger in her heart she uttered these words:
"Lord Phoibos, long distance archer, I shall put a word in your heart,
since you intend to build a beautiful temple in this place,
to be an oracle for men who will always
260   bring unblemished hecatombs to you.
Yet, the words I shall speak do put deep down in your heart.
Swift horses and mules will pound the ground
as they water at my sacred springs only to annoy you,
and men will prefer to gaze upon
265   the well-made chariots and the pounding, swift-footed horses
than upon the great temple and the many possessions therein.
But please listen to me—you are a lord better and mightier
than I am, and your power is very great—

build at Krisa beneath the fold of Parnassos.

270   There neither beautiful chariots will rattle nor swift-footed
horses will pound about the well-built altar.
But to you as Iêpaiêôn the glorious races of men
will bring gifts, and with delighted heart you will receive
beautiful sacrificial offerings from those dwelling about."

275   With these words Telphousa swayed his mind, so that hers alone,
and not the Far-shooter's, should be the glory of the land.
You soon left that place, O Far-shooting Apollon,
and reached the city of the Phlegyes, those insolent men,
who dwelt on this earth, with no regard for Zeus,

280   in a beautiful glen near the lake Kephisis.
From there you rushed to a mountain ridge,
and you reached Krisa beneath snowy Parnassos,
a foothill looking westwards, with a rock
hanging above it and a hollow and rough glen

285   running below it. There the lord Phoibos Apollon
resolved to make a lovely temple and spoke these words:
"Here I intend to build a beautiful temple
to be an oracle for men who shall always
bring unblemished hecatombs to this place;

290   and as many as dwell on fertile Peloponnesos
and on Europe and throughout the sea-girt islands
will consult it. It is my wish to give them unerring
advice, making prophecies inside the lavish temple."
With these words Phoibos Apollon laid out the foundations,

295   broad and very long from beginning to end; and on them
the sons of Erginos, Trophonios and Agamedes,
dear to the immortal gods, placed a threshold of stone.
And the numberless races of men built the temple all around
with hewn stones, to be a theme of song forever.

300   Near it there was a fair-flowing spring, where the lord,
son of Zeus, with his mighty bow, killed a she-dragon,
a great, glutted, and fierce monster, which inflicted
many evils on the men of the land—many on them
and many on their slender-shanked sheep; for she was bloodthirsty.

305   And once from golden-throned Hera she received and reared
dreadful and baneful Typhaôn, a scourge to mortals.
Hera gave birth to him in anger at father Zeus,
when the son of Kronos gave birth to glorious Athena
from his head; and mighty Hera was quickly angered

310   and spoke to the gathering of the immortal gods:

"All gods and all goddesses, hear from me
how cloud-gathering Zeus is first to dishonor me,
since he made me his mindfully devoted wife,
and now apart from me he gave birth to gray-eyed Athena,
315   who excels among all the blessed immortals.
But my son, Hephaistos, whom I myself bore
has grown to be weak-legged and lame among the blessed gods.
I took him with my own hands and cast him into the broad sea,
but Thetis, the silver-footed daughter of Nereus,
320   received him and with her sisters took him in her care.
I wish she had done the blessed gods some other favor!
O stubborn and wily one! What else will you now devise?
How dared you, alone, give birth to gray-eyed Athena?
Would not I have done that?—I, who was called your very own
325   among the immortal gods who dwell in the broad sky.
[325a Take thought now and fear that I might devise some evil for you in return!]
I shall contrive to have born to me
a child who will excel among the immortals.
To our sacred wedlock I shall bring no shame,
nor visit your bed, but I shall pass my time
330   far from you, among the immortals."
With these words she went apart from the gods very angry.
Then soon enough mighty, cow-eyed Hera prayed
and with the flat of her hand she struck the ground and spoke:
"Hear me now, Earth and broad Sky above,
335   and you Titans from whom gods and men are descended
and who dwell beneath the earth round great Tartaros.
Hearken to me, all of you, and apart from Zeus grant me a child,
in no way inferior in strength; nay, let him be stronger
than Zeus by as much as far-seeing Zeus is stronger than Kronos."
340   So she cried out and beat the earth with her stout hand.
Then the life-giving earth was moved and Hera saw it,
and her heart was delighted at the thought of fulfillment.
From then on, and until a full year came to its end,
she never came to the bed of contriving Zeus,
345   nor pondered for him sagacious counsels,
sitting as before on her elaborate throne,
but staying in temples, where many pray,
cow-eyed, mighty Hera delighted in the offerings she received.
When the months and the days reached their destined goal,
350   and the seasons arrived as the year revolved,
she gave birth to dreadful and baneful Typhaôn, a scourge to mortals,

whose aspect resembled neither gods' nor mortals'.
Soon cow-eyed, mighty Hera took him and, piling evil
upon evil, she commended him to the care of the she-dragon.
355 She worked many evils on the glorious races of men,
and she brought their day of doom to those who met her,
until the lord, Far-shooting Apollon, shot her
with a mighty arrow; rent with insufferable pains,
she lay panting fiercely and writhing on the ground.
360 The din was awe-inspiring, ineffably so, and throughout the forest
she rapidly thrust her coils all over; with a gasp
she breathed out her gory spirit, while Phoibos Apollon boasted:
"Rot now right here on the man-nourishing earth;
you shall not ever again be an evil bane for living men
365 who eat the fruit of the earth that nurtures many
and will bring to this place unblemished hecatombs,
nor shall Typhoeus or ill-famed Chimaira
ward off woeful death for you, but right here
the black earth and the flaming sun will make you rot."
370 So he spoke boasting, and darkness covered her eyes.
The holy fury of Helios made her rot away;
hence the place is now called Pythô, and people
call the lord by the name Pytheios, because on that spot
the relentless fury of Helios made the monster rot away.
375 At last Phoibos Apollon knew in his mind
why the fair-flowing spring had deceived him.
So in anger against Telphousa he set out and quickly reached her
and, standing very close to her, he uttered these words:
"Telphousa, you were not destined, after all, to deceive my mind
380 by keeping this lovely place to pour forth your fair-flowing water.
The glory of this place will be mine, too, not yours alone."
So spoke the lord, Far-shooting Apollon, and pushed down on her a cliff,
and with a shower of rocks he covered her streams;
then he built himself an altar in the wooded grove,
385 very close to the fair-flowing stream, and there all men
pray, calling upon him as the Telphousian lord,
because he shamed the streams of sacred Telphousa.
And then Phoibos Apollon pondered in his mind
what kind of men he should bring in to celebrate his rites
390 and be his ministers in rocky Pytho.
As he pondered these thoughts, he spotted a swift ship
on the wine-dark sea; there were many noble men on it,
Cretans from Minoan Knossos, who for the lord

make sacrificial offerings and proclaim the decrees
395   of Phoibos Apollon of the golden sword, whatever he may say
when he prophesies from the laurel below the dells of Parnassos.
To sandy Pylos and its native dwellers
they sailed in a black ship for barter and goods,
and Phoibos Apollon went to meet them at sea
400   and, looking like a dolphin in shape, he leapt on
the swift ship and lay on it like some great and awe-inspiring monster.
It entered no man's mind to know who he was
as he lunged about and shook the timbers of the ship.
They sat on the ship, afraid and dumbfounded,
405   and neither slacked the sheets of the hollow black ship
nor lowered the sail of the dark-prowed keel.
After they fixed its direction with oxhide lines,
they sailed on; a rushing tail wind pressed
the swift ship forward from behind. First sailing past Maleia
410   and then past the land of Lakonia, they reached
a sea-crowned city, a place of Helios who gladdens mortals,
Tainaron, where always graze the long-fleeced sheep
of lord Helios and are the tenants of the delightful place.
They wanted to put the ship to shore there and land
415   to contemplate the great portent and see with their own eyes
whether the monster would remain on the deck of the hollow ship
or leap into the briny swell, which teems with fish.
But the well-wrought ship did not obey the helm,
and off the shore of fertile Peloponnesos
420   went her way as the lord, Far-shooting Apollon, easily
steered her course with a breeze. She traversed her path
and reached Arênê and lovely Argyphea,
and Thyron, the ford of Alpheios, and well-built Aipy,
and sandy Pylos and its native dwellers.
425   She sailed past Krounoi and Chalkis and Dymê
and splendid Elis, where the Epeioi are lords.
When she was headed for Pherai, exulting in the tail wind
sent by Zeus, from under the clouds the lofty mountain of Ithakê
appeared, and Doulichion and Samê and wooded Zakynthos.
430   But when the shore of Peloponnesos was behind her,
and there loomed in the distance Krisa's boundless gulf,
which cuts off from the mainland the fertile Peloponnesos,
there blew decreed by Zeus a great and fair west wind
rushing down vehemently from the clear sky, so that the ship
435   might soon cross in speed the briny water of the sea.

Then they sailed back toward the dawn and the sun,
and lord Apollon, son of Zeus, was their leader
until they reached the harbor of conspicuous Krisa,
rich in vineyards, where the seafaring ship grounded on the sands.
440 And there the lord, Far-shooting Apollon, leaped from the ship,
like a star at midday, as flashes of light
flew about and their brilliance touched the sky.
Through the precious tripods he entered his temple
and lighted a flame to guide the ships,
445 enveloping all of Krisa in light; and the wives
and fair-girded daughters of the Krisians raised a cry
at the radiance of Phoibos, for he instilled in them great fear.
From there, swift as thought, he took a flying leap
back into the ship, in the form of a strong and vigorous
450 man in his prime, his mane covering his broad shoulders.
With a loud voice he uttered winged words:
"Who are you strangers and what harbor did you leave behind to sail the watery
    paths?
Is it perhaps for barter, or do you wander idly
over the sea like roaming pirates
455 who risk their lives to bring evil upon men of other lands?
Why do you sit this way in fear, neither going out
to shore nor stowing the tackle of your black ship?
Such indeed is the custom of men who work for their bread,
whenever on their black ship they approach land
460 from the sea, worn-out with toil, and straightway
a longing for sweet food grips their hearts."
So he spoke and put courage in their breasts,
and the leader of the Cretans spoke to him in answer:
"Stranger, since in no way do you resemble a mortal
465 in build or stature, but rather look like the deathless gods,
a hearty hail to you, may the gods grant you good fortune.
Now speak the truth to me that I may know well.
What folk is this, what land, what mortals live here?
With other designs in mind we sailed over the vast sea
470 to Pylos from Crete, whence we boast our race to hail.
Now against our will we have sailed here in our ship,
on another course and another path, and long to go home;
but some immortal has brought us here against our will."
Far-shooting Apollon spoke to them in reply:
475 "Strangers, up to now your homes were round Knossos
with its many trees; now you shall no longer be

on the homeward journey, bound for your lovely city,
your beautiful homes and dear wives, but you shall be in charge
of my lavish temple, which is honored by many men.
480 I am the son of Zeus and proudly declare I am Apollon.
I brought you here over the vast and deep sea,
entertaining no evil thoughts, but here you shall be keepers
of my lavish temple, which is greatly honored by all mortals,
and you shall know the will of the immortals, by whose wish
485 you shall be honored forever to the end of your days.
Come and obey at once whatever I say:
first slack the oxhide lines, lower the sails,
then draw the swift ship onto the land;
out of the well-trimmed keel take tackle and possessions,
490 and make an altar upon the beach of the sea;
then light a fire on it and offer white barley,
and, standing round the altar, say your prayers.
Since I, at first on the misty sea
in the form of a dolphin, leaped onto the swift ship,
495 pray to me as Delphinios, lord of dolphins; the altar, too,
shall be called Delphinian and be forever conspicuous.
After that have your meal by the swift black ship,
and pour libations to the blessed gods who dwell on Olympos.
When you have rid yourselves of desire for sweet food,
500 come with me, singing the Iêpaiêôn hymn,
until you reach the place where you shall care for my lavish temple."
So he spoke, and they readily listened to him and obeyed.
First they lowered the sails and slacked the oxhide lines,
and by the forestays brought the mast down to the mast-holder.
505 Then they themselves landed on the beach
and drew the swift ship from the sea onto the land,
and high onto the sand, and spread long props underneath.
There, on the beach they made an altar,
then lighted a fire on it, and with an offering of white barley
510 they prayed, as he ordered, standing round the altar.
They then had their meal by the swift black ship
and poured libations to the blessed gods who dwell on Olympos.
And when they rid themselves of the desire for food and drink,
they set out to go, and lord Apollon, son of Zeus, led the way,
515 his step high and stately, and with the lyre in his hands
he played a lovely tune. The Cretans followed him
to Pytho, beating time and singing the Iepaieon
in the fashion of Cretans singing a paean when the divine

Muse has put mellifluous song in their hearts.
520   They walked up the hill unwearied and soon reached
Parnassos and the lovely place where the god was destined
to dwell honored by many men; he led them there
and showed them the sacred sanctuary and lavish temple.
Their spirit was roused in their dear hearts,
525   and the leader of the Cretans put a question to him:
"Lord, since far from our beloved kin and our fatherland
you have brought us—for so it pleased your heart—
how are we now to live? Do tell us please!
This charming place does not abound in vineyards or meadows
530   from which we may live well and be in the service of men."
Apollon, son of Zeus, now smiled:
"Foolish men and poor wretches you are for preferring
cares and toilsome hardships and anguish for your hearts.
Put in your minds the word I will speak to set you at ease:
535   With a knife in his right hand let each one of you
slaughter sheep forever, and there will be an abundance
of them brought to me by the glorious races of men.
Guard my temple and receive the multitudes of mortals
gathered here, and especially my direction

.   .   .   .

540   If your word or deed shall be vain
and wantonly insolent, as is the custom of mortals,
then others will rule over you,
and by force be your masters forever.
I have told you everything; do keep it in your minds."
545   So, son of Zeus and Leto, farewell,
I shall remember you and another song as well.

4 : To Hermes

Of Hermes sing, O Muse, the son of Zeus and Maia,
lord of Kyllene and of Arcadia abounding with sheep,
helpful messenger of the immortals, to whom Maia gave birth,
the fair-tressed and revered nymph, when she found love in the arms of Zeus;
5   she shunned the company of the blessed gods
and lived inside a thick-shaded cave, where Kronion,
escaping the eyes of immortal gods and mortal men,
lay in love with the fair-tressed nymph in the darkness of night,
while sweet sleep overcame white-armed Hera.
10   But when the mind of great Zeus accomplished its goal,

and the tenth moon was set fast in the sky,
a newborn child saw the light, and uncanny deeds came to pass.
She gave birth to a child, a shrewd and coaxing schemer,
a cattle-rustling robber, and a bringer of dreams,
15   a watcher by night, and a gate-keeper, soon destined
to show forth glorious deeds among the immortal gods.
Born at dawn, by midday he played the lyre,
and at evening he stole the cattle of Far-shooting Apollon,
on the fourth of the month, the very day mighty Maia gave birth to him.
20   After he sprang forth from his mother's immortal limbs,
he did not remain for long lying in his holy cradle,
but he leaped up and searched for the cattle of Apollon,
stepping over the threshold of the high-roofed cave.
There he found a tortoise and won boundless bliss,
25   for Hermes was the first to make a singer of a tortoise,
which met him at the gates of the courtyard,
grazing on the lush grass near his dwelling
and dragging its straddling feet; the helpful son of Zeus
laughed when he saw it and straightway he said:
30   "Already an omen of great luck! I don't despise you.
Hail, O shapely hoofer and companion at the feast!
Your sight is welcome! Where is this lovely toy from,
a mountain tortoise, whose gleaming shell is now your armor?
I shall take you and bring you inside for handsome profit.
35   I shall not dishonor you for you will serve me first.
Better to be inside; being outdoors is harmful for you.
Indeed alive you shall be a charm against baneful
witchcraft; then again if you die, your song could be beautiful."
So he spoke and with both hands he lifted it up
40   and ran back into his abode, carrying the lovely toy.
There he tossed it upside down and with a chisel of gray iron
he scooped out the life of the mountain-turtle.
As when swift thought pierces the breast
of a man in whom thick-coming cares churn,
45   or as when flashing glances dart from quick-rolling eyes,
so glorious Hermes pondered word and deed at once.
He cut measured stalks of reed and fastened them
on the flesh of the animal, the scaly skin of the tortoise;
he skillfully stretched oxhide round the shell
50   and on it he fixed two arms joined by a crosspiece
from which he stretched seven harmonious strings of sheep-gut.
When it was finished, he held up the lovely toy

and with the plectrum struck it tunefully, and under his hand
the lyre rang awesome. The god sang to it beautifully,
55   as on the lyre he tried improvisations, such as young men do
at the time of feasts when they taunt and mock each other.
He sang of Zeus Kronides, also of Maia and even her beautiful sandals,
how they once flirted and dallied in the sweetness of love,
recounting in detail his own glorious birth.
60   He also praised the handmaidens, the splendid home of the nymph,
and the tripods throughout her dwelling, and the imperishable cauldrons.
That is what he sang, but other matters engaged his mind.
He carried the hollow lyre and laid it down
in the holy cradle, and then craving for meat
65   he leaped out of the fragrant dwelling and went forth scouting,
pondering some bold wile in his mind, such as men
who are bandits pursue when dark night falls.
Helios was plunging down from the earth into the ocean
with his horses and chariot, when Hermes in haste
70   reached the shaded mountains of Pieria,
where the divine cattle of the blessed gods had their stalls
and grazed on the lovely untrodden meadows.
Then the son of Maia, sharp-eyed Argeiphontes,
cut off from the herd fifty head of loud-lowing cattle.
75   Through sandy places he drove them on a beguiling route,
turning their hoofprints round. Master of the artful ruse,
he reversed their hooves, setting the front part backward
and the back part frontward and opposite to his own course.
Quickly on the sandy beach he wove sandals
80   of wicker-work, wondrous things of unimaginable skill,
plaiting tamarisk and twigs of myrtle.
He made a bundle of fresh-grown seasonable branches
and snugly tied them to be sandals for his feet,
leaves and all, just as glorious Argeiphontes
85   had plucked them from Pieria to lighten the toil of walking
by making his own device, as one does on an urgent long journey.
But an old man working on his flowering vineyard saw him,
as he pressed on toward the plain through grassy-bedded Onchestos.
The son of glorious Maia was first to address him:
90   "Bent-shouldered old man digging round your vines,
no doubt you shall have plenty of wine when all these bear fruit.
Be blind to what you saw and deaf to what you heard,
and silent too when no harm is done to what is your own."
This much said, the precious cattle he drove on,

95   and glorious Hermes led them through many shaded mountains,
ravines loud-echoing with blustering winds, and flowering plains.
Most of the wondrous night, his sable accomplice, had passed,
and dawn was soon to come and send people to work.
The shining Selene, daughter of lord Pallas,
100 son of Megamedes, had just mounted her watch-post,
when the doughty son of Zeus drove the wide-browed
cattle of Phoibos Apollon to the river Alpheios.
Not broken in, the cattle came to a high-roofed barn
and watering-troughs close to a remarkable meadow.
105 Then when he had grazed well the loud-lowing cattle,
he herded them together and drove them into the barn
while they were chewing lotus and dewy galingale,
and intent on the skill of making fire he fetched a lot of wood.
A fine branch of laurel he took and peeled with his knife

.   .   .   .

110 tight-fitted in his palm, and up went the heated smoke.
Hermes was the first to give us fire from fire-sticks.
He gathered many dry sticks and made a thick
and sturdy pile in a sunken pit; and the flame shone afar,
giving off a blast, as the fire burnt high.
115 While the power of glorious Hephaistos kindled the fire,
he dragged out to the door close by the fire
two curved-horned bellowing cows; indeed great was his strength.
They puffed as he cast them both on their backs,
and bending their necks he rolled them over and pierced their spines.
120 Task upon task he carried out and hacked the fatted meat.
He pierced with wooden spits and roasted
meat on prized bone and dark blood,
wrapped in guts all this; and heaped up on the spot.
The skins he stretched on a hard and dry rock
125 and up to this day and after all these years they are there,
an endlessly long time after those events; then
cheerful Hermes dragged the sumptuous meal
onto a smooth slab and chopped it into twelve portions
given by lot and to each he assigned perfect honor.
130 Then glorious Hermes craved for the sacred meat
because the sweet savor weakened his resolve, immortal though
he was. But not even so was his manly soul prevailed upon,
although his holy gullet greatly hankered for the meat.
But he stowed fat with much of the meat away
135 in the high-roofed barn and swiftly hung it up

as a token of his recent theft; then dry wood he gathered
and let the breath of the fire consume the shaggy feet and heads.
After the god accomplished everything in proper order,
he threw his sandals into the deep-eddying Alpheios;

140   he let the glowing embers die down and on the black ashes
strewed sand all night, as fair shone the light of Selene.
Then speedily he came back to Kyllene's shining peaks
at dawn, and no one met him on his long journey,
neither blessed god nor mortal man,

145   and no dog barked. And Hermes, the son of Zeus,
slipped through the keyhole of the dwelling sideways,
like autumnal breeze in outer form, or airy mist.
He made straight for the cave and reached its copious fane,
walking softly on his feet, not pounding as one might upon the ground.

150   Then glorious Hermes came to his cradle in haste,
and wrapped his swaddling clothes about his shoulders,
like an infant child, and lay there playing with the covers with palms
and thighs and keeping his sweet lyre to his left.
The god did not remain unnoticed by his divine mother who said:

155   "What is this, you weaver of schemes? Where are you coming from
in the dead of night clothed in shamelessness? I surely think
that either Leto's son will shackle your arms about your ribs
and drag you through the doorway,
or you will rove the gorges as a raiding bandit.

160   Go back! Your father planted you to be a vexing care
among mortal men and deathless gods."
Hermes spoke to her with sly intent:
"Mother, why do you fling these words at me as at an infant
who knows but a few wicked thoughts in his mind

165   and full of fear is cowed by his mother's chiding?
I shall be master of whatever skill is best
to provide for you and me forever; we shall not bear,
as you bid me, to stay right here and be
the only two immortals not pleased with gifts and prayers.

170   It is better to be forever in the gods' intimate circle,
rich, affluent, with an abundance of grain, than to sit
in this dark cave; and as for honor, I, too,
shall claim my share, much as Apollon does.
If my father does not allow me this, I shall surely

175   try to be, as I no doubt can, the chief of robbers.
If the son of glorious Leto searches for me,
then I think he will meet with some greater loss.

For to Pytho I shall go and break my way into his great house,
to plunder many beautiful tripods and cauldrons
180   and to take gold, too, and gleaming iron
and many garments; you shall witness this if you wish."
The son of aegis-bearing Zeus and mighty Maia
talked to each other this way.
Dawn, the early-born, was rising from deep-flowing Okeanos
185   to bring light to mortals, but Apollon
marched to Onchestos, the lovely and pure grove
of the loud-roaring Holder of the Earth. There, he found an old man
grazing his beast, the bulwark of his vineyard,
by the road, and the son of glorious Leto spoke to him first:
190   "Aged brambleberry-picker of grassy Onchestos,
I have come here from Pieria in search of my cattle,
all of them cows from my own herd,
every one with curved horns. The black bull was grazing alone
away from the rest and four hounds with flashing eyes,
195   like men sworn to a common scheme, followed them, but the hounds
and the bull were left behind, and this is truly a great wonder.
The sun had hardly set when they strayed away
from the soft meadow and the sweet pasture.
Aged man born of old, tell me whether you have seen
200   on this road a man going after my cows."
Now the old man replied to him and said:
"Friend, it is hard to tell all that one sees with his eyes;
for so many are the wayfarers traveling this road,
some of them bent on many evil things while others
205   go after what is good, and no easy task it is to know each one.
But I was digging round the hillock of my vineyard
all day long until the sun was setting;
and then, sir, I thought I saw a child—I can't be sure.
This child—an infant, too—followed the horned cows,
210   holding a staff and walking all about from side to side;
and he drove them with tails backwards and heads facing toward him."
So said the old man, and Apollon heard his words
and swiftly went his way. He saw a long-winged bird
and soon he knew that the robber was the son of Zeus Kronion.
215   Apollon, son of Zeus, speedily rushed
to holy Pylos in search of his shambling cows,
his broad shoulders enveloped in a purple cloud.
The Far-shooter saw the tracks and uttered these words:
"Heavens! A truly great wonder I see with my eyes.

220   These no doubt are the tracks of straight-horned cows,
      but they are turned backwards toward the flowery meadow.
      These tracks belong neither to man nor to woman,
      nor yet to gray wolves, nor bears, nor lions.
      Indeed, I do not think they are those of a shaggy-maned centaur—
225   who has taken such monstrous swift strides.
      Wondrous on this side of the road, they are yet more wondrous on the other side."
      With these words lord Apollon, son of Zeus, rushed
      and reached Mount Kyllene, overgrown with trees,
      and the deep-shaded, rocky hiding place where the divine
230   nymph gave birth to the son of Zeus Kronion.
      A delightful odor permeated the holy mountain,
      and many long-shanked sheep grazed on the grass.
      Then Apollon himself in haste stepped down
      the stone threshold and into the gloomy cave.
235   When Zeus's and Maia's son saw Apollon,
      the Far-shooter, angered about his cattle,
      he snuggled into his sweet-scented swaddling-clothes;
      and as ashes cover a heap of embers from tree-trunks,
      so Hermes wrapped himself up when he saw the Far-shooter.
240   Into a small space he huddled head, hands, and feet,
      like a freshly-bathed baby courting sweet sleep,
      but in truth still awake and holding the lyre under his arm.
      The son of Zeus and Leto did not fail to recognize
      the beautiful mountain nymph and her dear son,
245   though he was a tiny child steeped in crafty wiles.
      He peered into every niche and nook of the great dwelling,
      and he took a shining key and opened three vaults
      filled with nectar and lovely ambrosia;
      inside them lay much gold and silver
250   and the many purple and silver-white garments of the nymph,
      such as the holy dwellings of the blessed gods contain.
      Then when he had searched the recesses of the great dwelling,
      the son of Leto spoke these words to glorious Hermes:
      "Child lying in the cradle, hurry up and tell me about the cows!
255   Else you and I will soon part not like two friends.
      I will cast you down and hurl you into gloomy Tartaros
      and into dread and inescapable darkness; and neither your mother
      nor your father will restore you to light but beneath the earth
      you shall wander as lord of tiny babyfolk."
260   Hermes spoke to him with cunning words:
      "Son of Leto, are not these harsh words you have spoken?

And are you here in search of roving cattle?
I have neither seen, nor found out, nor heard another man's word;
so I will neither tell, nor get the reward for telling.

265 I surely do not resemble a hardy rustler of cattle,
and this is no deed of mine, as I have cared for other matters;
I have cared for sleep, and milk from my mother's breast,
and for swaddling-clothes wrapped round my shoulders, and a warm bath.
May no one find out how this quarrel came to be!

270 For it would be a great wonder among the immortals
how a newborn baby passed through the doorway
with cattle pasturing in the fields; the claim is preposterous!
I was born yesterday, and the ground is too rough on my soft feet.
If you wish, I will swear by my father's head—and this is a great oath.

275 I vow that I myself am not the culprit
and that I have seen no one else steal your cows—
whatever these cows are; I hear only rumors."
So he spoke and, with many a darting glance,
he moved his eyebrows up and down and looked here and there;

280 and with a long whistle he listened to the story as to an idle tale.
Far-shooting Apollon laughed gently and spoke to him:
"Friend, I do think you are a scheming rogue,
and judging from the way you talk you must often have broken into
well-built houses and stripped many men of their possessions,

285 as you quietly packed away their belongings.
You will be a pain to many shepherds dwelling outdoors
in mountain glades, when you come upon their herds of cattle
and fleecy sheep, driven by a craving for meat.
But come, for fear that this might be your last and final sleep,

290 come down from the cradle, you comrade of dark night.
From now on you shall have this honor among the immortals,
to be called the chief of robbers all your days."
With these words Phoibos Apollon took up and carried the child.
And then mighty Argeiphontes pondered in his mind

295 and, as he was lifted in Apollon's arms, he sent forth an omen,
a hardy effort of the belly and a reckless messenger.
And on top of that he swiftly sneezed; and Apollon
heard all this and dropped glorious Hermes down on the ground.
Although he was intent on his journey, he sat beside him

300 and, chiding Hermes, he spoke to him with these words:
"Never fear, swathed child of Zeus and Maia.
Even later I shall find the precious cows
by these omens, and you shall lead the way."

So he spoke, and Kyllenian Hermes sprang up swiftly
305 and moved in haste; he pushed back his ears with his hands
and, his swaddling clothes wrapped about his shoulders, he said:
"Whither are you carrying me, Far-shooter, mightiest of all the gods?
Are you annoying me because you are so angry about the cows?
Oh my! I wish every single cow would perish!
310 Surely I neither stole the cows—whatever cows are—
nor saw another man do it. Rumor is all I hear!
Let Zeus Kronion be the judge and accept his verdict."
And after Hermes the shepherd and the glorious son of Leto
questioned each other on every point clearly
315 and still did not agree, Apollon spoke a truthful word.

. . . .

Not unjustly did he seize glorious Hermes for stealing
the cows, but the Kyllenian with wheedling words and artful tricks
wanted to deceive the lord of the silver bow.
When, though many were his own wiles, he found
320 Apollon full of matching schemes, then he speedily led the way
across the sand, while the son of Zeus and Leto followed.
The beautiful children of Zeus soon reached
the peak of fragrant Olympos and their father, Kronion;
for there the scales of justice were set for both.
325 A pleasant chatter filled snowy Olympos
as ageless immortals gathered after golden-throned dawn.
Then Hermes and Apollon of the silver bow stood
before the knees of Zeus, and loud-thundering Zeus
spoke to his illustrious son and questioned him:
330 "Phoibos, where did you find this welcome booty,
a newborn child who looks like a herald?
A weighty matter has come before the divine assembly."
Then the Far-shooting lord, Apollon, replied:
"Father, since you reproach me for being the only one
335 fond of booty, you shall soon hear a mighty story.
After a long journey to the mountains of Kyllene
I found a child, a burgling looter
with sharpness of tongue such as I have seen in neither god
nor mortal, among those who cheat people on this earth.
340 He stole my cows from the meadow and drove them away;
he went along the shore of the resounding sea,
and headed straight for Pylos; there were monstrous footprints
of two kinds, such are a noble god's wondrous works.
As for the cows, the black dust kept and showed

345 their footprints reversed in the direction of the flowery meadow.
He himself—irrepressible fellow that he is—
walked over the sand neither on his feet nor on his hands.
But with some other contrivance he left
such monstrous tracks behind, as if he walked on stilts.

350 So long as he drove the cattle over sandy ground,
the tracks stood out clearly in the sand.
But when he came to the end of the great sandy stretch,
his own tracks and those of the cows became invisible
on the hard ground. But a mortal man saw him

355 as he drove the wide-browed kine straight to Pylos.
And after he had penned up the cows quietly
and, alternating roadsides, craftily made his way home,
he lay in his cradle, looking like the black night
in the darkness of the gloomy cave; and not even

360 a sharp-eyed eagle would have spotted him. With his hands
he rubbed his eyes and nursed wily thoughts,
and soon he uttered these reckless words:
'I have neither seen, nor found out, nor heard another man's word,
and I shall neither tell, nor get the reward for telling.'"

365 Phoibos Apollon spoke these words and then sat down.
Hermes now addressed Kronion, lord of all the gods,
and told the immortals quite another story:
"Father Zeus, I shall speak the truth to you,
for I am all for the truth and know not how to lie.

370 He came to our place in search of his shambling cows
today, only a little after the sun had risen,
and brought none of the blessed gods as eyewitness or deponent.
He applied much force and ordered me to confess,
and often threatened to cast me down to broad Tartaros,

375 just because he is in the tender bloom of glorious youth
while I was born but yesterday; he knows all this himself,
for in no way do I resemble a rough man and a cattle-rustler.
Believe me—after all, you claim to be my dear father—
I did not drive his cows to my house and—bless me—

380 I did not cross over the threshold. This is the whole truth.
I greatly reverence Helios and the other gods,
and I love you and stand in awe of him. You do know
that I am not guilty, and now I take a great oath:
No! By these well-decked porticoes of the immortals!

385 Someday I will pay him back for this heartless inquiry,
stronger though he is; but come to the aid of younger folk."

So spoke Kyllenian Argeiphontes with a coy look
and held his swaddling clothes fast on his arm.
Zeus laughed out loud when he heard the mischievous child
390 deny so well and so adroitly any connection with the cattle.
He ordered them both to come to an accord
and search for the cattle, and Hermes to guide and lead the way
and in all good faith to show the place
where he had hidden away the precious cattle.
395 Then Kronides nodded with his head and illustrious Hermes obeyed,
for the mind of aegis-bearing Zeus easily commanded obedience.
The beautiful children of Zeus both hurried away
to sandy Pylos and came to the ford of Alpheios.
They reached the fields and the high-roofed barn
400 where the animals were pampered at nighttime.
Then Hermes went to the rocky cave
and drove out of it the precious cattle.
Apollon looked aside and noticed the cowhides
on a steep rock, and quickly asked glorious Hermes:
405 "How could you, you clever rogue, have slaughtered two cows,
being still a newborn infant? Even I myself
look back and admire your strength; no need for you
to grow up for long, O Kyllenian son of Maia."
So he spoke, and with his hand he twisted mighty shackles
410 made of withes. But they swiftly took root into the earth
and under his feet, as though grafted onto that spot,
and easily entwined each other and all the roving cows,
by the will of thievish Hermes, as Apollon
gazed in wonder. Then mighty Argeiphontes,
415 fire darting from his eyes, looked askance at the ground

. . . .

longing to hide. Then he easily soothed the Far-shooting
son of glorious Leto, exactly as he wished,
mightier though Apollon was. Upon his left arm he took
the lyre and with the plectrum struck it tunefully and under his hand
420 resounded an awe-filled sound. And Phoibos Apollon laughed
for joy as the lovely sound of the divine music
went through to his heart and sweet longing seized him
as he listened attentively. Playing sweetly on the lyre,
the son of Maia boldly stood to the left
425 of Phoibos Apollon and to the clear-sounding lyre
he sang as one sings preludes. His voice sounded lovely,
as he sang of the immortal gods and of black earth,

how they came to be, and how each received his lot.
Of the gods with his song he first honored Mnemosyne,
430   mother of the Muses, for the son of Maia fell to her lot.
The glorious son of Zeus honored the immortals,
according to age, and as each one had been born,
singing of everything in due order as he played the lyre on his arm.
A stubborn longing seized Apollon's heart in his breast,
435   and with winged words he spoke to him:
"Scheming cattle-slayer, industrious comrade of the feast,
your performance is worth fifty cows;
I think we will settle our accounts at peace.
But come now, tell me, inventive son of Maia,
440   have these wondrous deeds followed you from birth,
or has some mortal man or deathless god
given you this glorious gift and taught you divine song?
Wondrous is this new-uttered sound I hear,
and such as I think no man or deathless god
445   dwelling on Olympos has ever yet learned,
except for you, O robber, son of Zeus and Maia.
What skill is this? What music for inescapable cares?
What virtuosity? For surely here are three things to choose
all at once: good cheer, love, and sweet sleep.
450   I, too, am a follower of the Olympian Muses,
who cherish dance, the glorious field of song,
festive chant, and the lovely resonance of flutes.
But no display of skill by young men at a feast
has ever touched my heart in this manner.
455   Son of Zeus, I marvel at your charm when you play the lyre.
Now, though you are little, your ideas are remarkable;
sit down, friend, and have regard for the words of your elders.
There will indeed be renown for you among the immortals,
for you and your mother. I shall be clear:
460   yes, by the cornel spear, I shall truly make you
a glorious and thriving leader among the immortals,
and I shall give you splendid gifts without deception to the end."
Hermes replied to him with cunning words:
"You question me carefully, Far-shooter, and I
465   do not begrudge your becoming master of my skill.
You shall know it today. I want to be gentle to you
in my words of advice—your mind knows all things well.
For, noble and mighty as you are, O son of Zeus, your seat
is first among the immortals, and wise Zeus loves you,

470   by every sacred right, and has granted you splendid gifts.
     They say, O Far-shooter, that from Zeus and his divine voice
     you learned the ranks, the prophet's skills, and all god-given revelations.
     I myself have come to know that you have all these in abundance.
     You may choose to learn whatever you will,
475   but since your heart longs to play the lyre,
     sing and play the lyre and tend joyous festivities;
     receive this skill from me and, friend, grant me glory.
     Sing well with this clear-voiced mistress in your arms,
     since you have the gift of beautiful and proper speech.
480   From now on in carefree spirit bring it to the well-provided feast,
     the lovely dance, and the revel where men vie for glory,
     as a fountain of good cheer day and night.
     Whoever with skill and wisdom expertly asks,
     to him it will speak and teach him all manner of things
485   joyful to the mind, being played with a gentle touch,
     for it shuns toilsome practice. But if anyone should
     in ignorance question it at first with rudeness,
     to him in vain it will chatter high-flown gibberish forever.
     You may choose to learn whatever you desire;
490   I will make a gift of it to you, glorious son of Zeus.
     For my part, O Far-shooter, I will graze the roving cattle
     on the pastures of the mountain and the horse-nurturing plain,
     where cows are mounted by bulls to give birth
     to males and females at random. And though your mind
495   is set on profit, there is no need for you to rage with anger."
     With these words he offered him the lyre, and Apollon took it,
     and put in Hermes's hand a shining whip,
     and commanded him to be a cowherd. The son of Maia accepted it
     joyfully. And the glorious son of Leto, Far-shooting
500   lord Apollon upon his left arm took the lyre
     and struck it tunefully with the plectrum. It resounded
     awesomely under his hand, and the god sang to it with grace.
     Then both of them turned the cows toward
     the divine meadow, and the beautiful children of Zeus
505   rushed to return to snowy Olympos,
     delighting in the lyre; and thus wise Zeus rejoiced
     and brought them together in friendship. For his part, Hermes
     always loved the son of Leto as he does even now,
     and he gave the lovely lyre as a keepsake
510   to the Far-shooter, who played it on his arm expertly.
     Hermes did invent the skill of a new art,

for he made the blaring pipes that can be heard from afar.
And then the son of Leto addressed Hermes:
"Son of Maia, crafty guide, I fear you might
515 steal back my lyre and the curved bow.
For it is your Zeus-given privilege to tend to
barter among the men of this nourishing earth;
but if you would deign to swear the great oath of the gods,
either by a nod of your head, or by the potent water of the Styx,
520 your deeds would be gracious and dear to my heart."
Then the son of Maia with a nod of his head promised
never to steal away whatever the Far-shooter possessed,
and never to approach his sturdy house. Then Apollon,
the son of Leto, for the sake of Hermes's friendship, vowed
525 that no one else among the immortals to him would be dearer,
neither god nor man descended from Zeus. And a perfect

. . . .

"contract among all the immortals I shall offer you,
one honored and trusted by my heart. And later
I shall give you a beautiful staff that brings bliss and wealth,
530 a golden one with three branches, to protect you against harm,
and to accomplish all the laws of noble words and deeds,
which I profess to know from the voice of Zeus.
Mightiest one and cherished by Zeus, it is not divine will
for you or any other immortal to know the divination
535 you inquire of. The mind of Zeus knows this.
I pledged and agreed and then swore a mighty oath
that, except for me, none of the eternal gods
would know the inscrutable will of Zeus.
And you, my brother of the golden wand, do not ask me
540 to show the divine decrees that far-seeing Zeus ponders.
To some men I will bring harm and to others benefit
as I herd the wretched tribes of men about.
My utterance will bring blessings to those who come
guided by the voice and flight of birds of sure omen.
545 No deception for him; he will profit from what I utter.
But whoever puts faith in the idle chatter of birds
and wishes to pry into my divination, against my designs,
and to understand more than the eternal gods,
makes his journey in vain; yet his gifts I shall take.
550 Now, son of glorious Maia and Zeus who holds
the aegis, helpful genius of the gods, I will tell you
another story: there are three awesome sisters,

virgins, delighting in their swift wings.
Their heads are besprinkled with white barley flour,
555   and they dwell under the fold of Parnassos,
apart from me, as teachers of divination, which I studied
when as a mere child I tended the cows, and my father
did not mind. From there flying now here, now there,
they feed on honeycomb and bring each thing to pass.
560   And after they eat yellow honey, they are seized
with mantic frenzy and are eager to speak the truth.
But if they are robbed of the sweet food of the gods,
then they do buzz about in confusion and they lie.
They are yours to question them thoroughly,
565   and to delight your heart; and if you are a mortal man's teacher,
he will often listen to you if good fortune is his.
Keep these, son of Maia, and the roving, curved-horned cattle
and tend horses and hardy mules."

. . . .

He commanded glorious Hermes to be lord over
570   lions with flashing eyes and boars with gleaming tusks,
and dogs, and all herds, and sheep fed by the broad earth;
and to be appointed sole messenger to Hades,
who, though implacable, will give no small prize.
Lord Apollon showed his love for the son of Maia
575   with every kind of affection, and Kronion bestowed grace upon him.
He is a companion to all immortals and all mortals.
Little is the profit he brings, as he beguiles endlessly
the tribes of mortal men throughout the night.
Farewell, son of Zeus and Maia;
580   I shall now remember you and another song as well.

5 : To Aphrodite

Sing to me, O Muse, of the deeds of golden Aphrodite,
the Cyprian, who stirs sweet longing in gods
and subdues the races of mortals as well as of birds
that swoop down from the sky and of all the beasts
5   that are nurtured in their multitudes on both land and sea.
Every one of them is affected by the deeds of fair-wreathed Kythereia.
Three are the minds of the goddesses she can neither sway nor deceive:
first is the daughter of aegis-bearing Zeus, gray-eyed Athena.
The deeds of Aphrodite the golden bring no pleasure to her,
10   but Athena finds joy in wars, in the work of Ares,

in the strife of battle, and in tending to deeds of splendor.
She was first to teach the craftsmen of this earth
how to make carriages and chariots with complex designs of bronze.
She taught splendid works to soft-skinned maidens,
15 in their houses, placing skill in each one's mind.
Second is hallooing Artemis of the golden shafts,
whom smile-loving Aphrodite can never tame in love.
She delights in the bow and in slaying mountain beasts,
in the lyre and the dance and in shrill cries
20 in shaded groves and in the city of just men.
Third is a revered maiden not charmed by the deeds of Aphrodite,
Hestia, whom Kronos of the crooked counsels begat first
and youngest too, by the will of aegis-bearing Zeus.
Poseidon and Apollon courted this mighty goddess
25 but she was unwilling and constantly refused.
She touched the head of aegis-bearing Zeus
and swore a great oath, which has been brought to pass,
that she, the illustrious goddess, would remain a virgin forever.
Instead of marriage, Zeus the father gave her a fair prize,
30 and she took the choicest boon and sat in the middle of the house.
In all the temples of the gods she has her share of honor
and for all mortals she is of all gods the most venerated.
Of these three she can neither sway the mind, nor deceive them.
But none of the others, neither blessed god
35 nor mortal, has escaped Aphrodite.
She even led astray the mind of Zeus who rejoices in thunder
and who is the greatest and has the highest honor.
Even his wise mind she tricks when she wills it
and easily mates him with mortal women,
40 making him forget Hera, his wife and sister,
by far the most beautiful among the deathless goddesses
and the most illustrious child to issue from crafty Kronos
and mother Rhea, whom Zeus, knower of indestructible plans,
made his modest and prudent wife.
45 Even in Aphrodite's soul Zeus placed sweet longing
to mate with a mortal man; his purpose was that even she
might not be kept away from a mortal's bed for long,
and that someday the smile-loving goddess might not
laugh sweetly and boast among all the gods
50 of how she had joined in love gods to mortal women,
who bore mortal sons to the deathless gods,
and of how she had paired goddesses with mortal men.

And so he placed in her heart sweet longing for Anchises
who, blessed with a god's handsome looks,
55   tended cattle on the towering peaks of Ida, rich in springs.
When indeed smile-loving Aphrodite saw him,
she fell in love, and a powerful longing seized her heart.
She went to Cyprus and entered her sweet-smelling temple
at Paphos, where her precinct and balmy temple are.
60   There she entered and behind her closed the shining doors;
the Graces bathed her and anointed her
with ambrosian oil such as is rubbed on deathless gods,
divinely sweet, and made fragrant for her sake.
After she clothed her body with beautiful garments
65   and decked herself with gold, smile-loving Aphrodite
left fragrant Cyprus behind and rushed toward Troy,
moving swiftly on a path high up in the clouds.
She reached Ida, rich in springs, mother of beasts,
and over the mountain she made straight for the stalls.
70   Along with her, fawning, dashed gray wolves
and lions with gleaming eyes and bears and swift leopards,
ever hungry for deer. When she saw them, she was delighted
in her heart and placed longing in their breasts,
so that they lay together in pairs along the shady glens.
75   She herself reached the well-built shelters
and found the hero Anchises, whose handsome looks were divine,
left alone and away from the others, by the stalls.
Everyone else followed the cattle on the grassy pastures,
but he was left alone by the stalls, and away from the others
80   he moved about and played a loud and clear lyre.
Aphrodite, the daughter of Zeus, stood before him,
in size and form like an unwed maiden,
so that he might not see who she was and be afraid.
When Anchises saw her, he pondered and marveled
85   at her size and form, and at her sparkling garments.
She was clothed in a robe more brilliant than gleaming fire
and wore spiral bracelets and shining earrings,
while round her tender neck there were beautiful necklaces,
lovely, golden, and of intricate design. Like the moon's
90   was the radiance round her soft breasts, a wonder to the eye.
Desire seized Anchises, and to her he uttered these words:
"Lady, welcome to this house, whoever of the blessed ones you are:
whether you are Artemis, or Leto, or golden Aphrodite,
or well-born Themis, or gray-eyed Athena.

95   You could be one of the Graces, who with all
      the gods keep company and are called immortal,
      perhaps one of the nymphs who haunt these lovely woods,
      or one of those who dwell on this imposing mountain
      in the streams of rivers and in the grassy dells.
100   Upon a lofty peak, which can be seen from all around,
      I shall make you an altar and offer you fair sacrifices
      in all seasons. With kindly heart grant me
      to be a great man among the Trojans,
      to leave flourishing offspring behind me,
105   and to behold the light of the sun for a long time,
      prospering among the people, and so reach the threshold of old age."
      Aphrodite, the daughter of Zeus, replied:
      "Anchises, most glorious of all men born on earth,
      I surely am no goddess; why do you liken me to the immortals?
110   A mortal am I, and born of a mortal woman.
      Renowned Otreus is my father—have you perhaps heard of his name?—
      who is lord over all of well-fortified Phrygia.
      I know well both my language and yours,
      for a Trojan nurse reared me in my house; she took me
115   from my dear mother and devotedly cared for me when I was little.
      This is why I know your language too.
      But now Argeiphontes of the golden wand carried me off
      from the dance of hallooing Artemis of the golden shafts.
      Many of us nymphs and maidens, worth many cows to our parents,
120   were playing, and endless was the crowd encircling us.
      From there Argeiphontes of the golden wand abducted me
      and carried me over the many labors of mortal men,
      over much undivided and uninhabited land, where beasts
      that eat raw flesh roam through the shady glens,
125   and I thought that my feet would never again touch the life-giving earth.
      He said I should be called your wedded wife, Anchises,
      and sharing your bed should bear you fine children.
      But once mighty Argeiphontes had explained this to me,
      he went away and joined the tribes of the immortals;
130   so I am before you because my need is compelling.
      By Zeus and by your noble parents I beseech you,
      for lowly ones could not bear offspring like you.
      Take me untouched and innocent of love,
      show me to your father, and wise mother,
135   also to your brothers born of the same womb;
      I shall be no unseemly daughter and sister.

Quickly send a messenger to the Phrygians, owners of swift horses,
to bring word to my father and to my mother in her grief;
they will send you much gold and many woven garments,

140   all splendid rewards I ask you to accept.
Once these things are done, prepare the lovely marriage feast,
which is honored by both men and immortal gods."
With these words the goddess placed sweet desire in his heart,
so that love seized Anchises and he spoke to her:

145   "If you are mortal and born of a mortal woman
and Otreus is your father, famous by name, as you say,
and if you are come here by the will of Hermes,
the immortal guide, you shall be called my wife forever.
And so neither god nor mortal man will restrain me

150   till I find love in your arms
right now; not even if Far-shooting Apollon himself
should let grievous arrows fly from his silver bow.
Godlike woman, willingly would I go to the house of Hades
once I have shared your bed."

155   With these words he took her by the hand; smile-loving Aphrodite,
turning her face away, with beautiful eyes downcast, went coyly
to the well-made bed, which was already laid
with soft coverings for its lord.
On it were skins of bears and deep-roaring lions,

160   which he himself had killed on the high mountains.
When they climbed onto the well-wrought bed,
first Anchises took off the bright jewels from her body,
brooches, spiral bracelets, earrings, and necklaces,
and loosed her girdle, and her brilliant garments

165   he stripped off and laid upon a silver-studded seat.
Then by the will of the gods and destiny he, a mortal,
lay beside a goddess, without knowing this fact.
And at the hour shepherds bring their oxen and flocks of sturdy sheep
back to the stalls from the flowering pastures,

170   she poured sweet sleep over Anchises
and clothed her body in her beautiful clothes.
When the noble goddess dressed in beautiful clothes,
she stood by the couch; her head touched the well-made roof-beam
and her cheeks were radiant with divine beauty,

175   such as belongs to fair-wreathed Kythereia.
Then she roused him from sleep and called him by his name:
"Rise, son of Dardanus! Why do you sleep so deeply?
Consider whether I look the same

as when you first saw me with your eyes."
180   So she spoke, and he obeyed her quickly and arose from sleep.
When he saw Aphrodite's neck and lovely eyes,
he was seized with fear and turned his gaze aside.
Then with his cloak he covered his handsome face
and spoke to her winged words in prayer:
185   "Goddess, as soon as I laid my eyes on you
I knew you were divine; but you did not tell the truth.
Yet by aegis-bearing Zeus I beseech you
not to let me live impotent among men,
but have pity on me; for the man who lies
190   with immortal goddesses is not left unharmed."
Aphrodite the daughter of Zeus answered him:
"Anchises, most glorious of mortal men,
courage! Have no fear at all in your heart.
No need to be afraid that you may suffer harm from me
195   or from the other blessed ones; the gods do love you.
You shall have a dear son who will rule over the Trojans,
and to his offspring children shall always be born.
Aineias—the Awesome One—his name shall be,
because I was seized with awful distress for sharing the bed of a mortal.
200   But of all mortal men your race is always
closest to the gods in looks and stature.
Wise Zeus abducted fair-haired Ganymedes
for his beauty, to be among the immortals
and pour wine for the gods in the house of Zeus;
205   he is a marvel to look upon, honored by all the gods,
as from the golden bowl he draws red nectar.
Relentless grief seized the heart of Tros, nor did he know
where the divine whirlwind had carried off his dear son.
So afterwards he wept for him unceasingly;
210   Zeus pitied him and gave him high-stepping horses,
such as carry the immortals, as a reward for his son.
He gave them as a gift to him to keep, and guiding
Argeiphontes at the behest of Zeus told him in detail
how his son would be immortal and ageless like the gods.
215   When he heard Zeus's message,
he no longer wept but rejoiced in his heart
and was gladly carried by the galloping horses.
So, too, golden-throned Eos abducted Tithonos,
one of your own race, who resembled the immortals.
220   She went to ask Kronion, lord of dark clouds,

to grant him immortality and never-ending life.
Zeus nodded assent and fulfilled her wish.
Mighty Eos was too foolish to think of asking
for the gift of immortality and exemption from baneful old age.
225   Indeed, so long as much-coveted youth was his,
he took his delight in early-born, golden-throned Eos,
and lived by the stream of Okeanos at the ends of the earth.
When the first gray hairs began to flow down
from his comely head and noble chin,
230   mighty Eos did refrain from his bed,
though she kept him in her house and pampered him
with food and ambrosia and gifts of fine clothing.
When detested old age weighed heavy on him
so he could move or lift none of his limbs,
235   this is the counsel that seemed best in her heart:
she placed him in a chamber and shut its shining doors.
His voice flows endlessly and there is no strength,
such as there was before, in his crooked limbs.
If this were to be your lot among immortals, I should not choose
240   for you immortality and eternal life.
But should you live on such as you now are
in looks and build, and be called my husband,
then no grief would enfold my prudent heart.
Yet you will soon be enveloped by leveling old age,
245   that pitiless companion of every man,
baneful, wearisome, and hated even by the gods.
Alas, great shame shall be mine among the immortal gods
to the end of all time because of you.
Till now they feared my scheming tattle,
250   by which, soon or late, I mated all immortal gods
to mortal women, for my will tamed them all.
This time I will not bear to mention this
among the immortals because, struck by great madness
in a wretched and grave way, and driven out of my mind,
255   I mated with a mortal and conceived a child beneath my girdle.
As soon as this child sees the light of the sun,
the full-bosomed mountain nymphs who dwell
on this great and holy mountain will nurture him.
They do not take after either mortals or immortals;
260   they live long and their food is like that of the immortal gods
and among the immortals they move nimbly in the beautiful dance.
The Seilenoi and sharp-eyed Argeiphontes

find love in their arms in caves where desire lurks.
When they are born, firs and towering oaks
265 spring up on the rich soil of the earth
and grow into lush beauty on the high mountains.
They stand lofty, and are called sanctuaries
of the gods; and mortals do not fell them with the ax.
Whenever fated death is near at hand,
270 first these beautiful trees wither and collapse on the ground,
the bark all around them shrivels up, the branches fall away,
and their souls and those of the nymphs leave the light of the sun together.
They will keep my son and nurture him.
As soon as he reaches much-coveted adolescence,
275 the goddesses will bring the child here to show him to you.
Here is what I have in mind,
toward the fifth year I will come to present our son to you.
When you first lay your eyes upon this blossom,
you will delight in the sight, for so much like a god he will be;
280 and you shall take him quickly to windy Ilion.
If any mortal should ask you
what sort of mother carried your dear son under her girdle,
do remember to speak to him as I bid you:
'He is the son, they say, of a nymph with a petal-soft face,
285 one of those who dwell on this forest-covered mountain.'
But if you reveal this and boast with foolish heart
to have found love in the arms of fair-wreathed Kythereia,
an angry Zeus will smite you with a smoking thunderbolt.
I have told you everything; with this clear in your mind,
290 refrain from naming me, and heed divine anger."
With these words she darted up to the windy sky.
Hail, O goddess and queen of well-settled Cyprus!
I began with you and I shall now go to another hymn.

6 : To Aphrodite

Of revered gold-wreathed and stunnning Aphrodite
I shall sing, to whose domain belong the battlements
of all sea-laved Cyprus where, blown by the moist breath of Zephyros,
she was carried over the waves of the resounding sea
5   in soft foam. The golden-crowned Horae
happily welcomed her and clothed her with heavenly raiment.
Then on her divine head they placed a well-wrought crown,
beautiful and golden, and in her pierced ears

flowers of brass and precious gold.

10   Round her soft neck and silver-white breasts
they decked her with golden necklaces such as the gold-filleted
Horae themselves are adorned with wherever they go
to the lovely dances of the gods and to their father's house.
After they decked her body with every sort of jewel,

15   they brought her to the immortals, who saw and welcomed her,
with open arms, as each one wished
that he might take her home as his wedded wife;
for they marveled at the looks of violet-crowned Kythereia.
Hail, honey-sweet goddess of the fluttering eyelids!

20   Grant me victory in this contest and arrange my song.
I shall remember you and another song as well.

7 : To Dionysos

I shall recall to mind how Dionysos, son of glorious Semele,
appeared on the shore of the barren sea,
on a jutting headland, looking like a young man
in the first bloom of manhood. His beautiful dark hair

5   danced about him, and on his stout shoulders he wore
a purple cloak. Soon on a well-benched ship
pirates moved forward swiftly on the wine-dark sea;
they were Tyrsenians led by an evil doom. When they saw him
they signaled to each other and then leapt out and quickly seized him

10   and put him on board their ship, glad in their hearts.
They thought he was the son of a Zeus-cherished king
and wanted to bind him with painful shackles.
But the shackles could not hold him and the withes fell far away
from his hands and feet; and he sat there smiling and dark-eyed.

15   When the helmsman perceived what this meant,
he quickly called upon his shipmates and said:
"Why do you seize and bind this mighty god, you crazy men?
Our well-made ship cannot even carry him!
He is either Zeus or Apollon of the silver bow,

20   or Poseidon, because he looks not like a mortal
but like a god who has his home on Olympos.
But come! Let us leave him upon the black mainland
at once! Do not lay hands on him; he might be angered
and he might raise violent winds and a great storm."

25   So he spoke, but the captain scolded him with harsh words:
"Madman! Keep your mind on the tail wind, and hold all the lines

and hoist the sails of the ship. The men will take care of him.
I reckon Egypt or Cyprus is his destination,
or the Hyperboreans or yet some more distant land.
30   When we are through with him he will talk about his friends
and brothers, and all his goods, since some god has sent him our way."
This said, he hoisted mast and sail on the ship,
and the wind blew the mainsail full as they pulled the lines
tight on both sides. But soon wondrous deeds unfolded before their eyes:
35   first throughout the swift black ship sweet and fragrant wine
formed a gurgling stream and a divine smell
arose as all the crew watched in mute wonder.
And next on the topmost sail a vine spread about,
all over, and many grapes were hanging down
40   in clusters. Then round the mast dark ivy twined,
luxuriant with flowers and lovely growing berries;
the thole-pins were crowned with wreaths. When they saw this
they ordered the helmsman to put the ship to shore.
Now the god became a fearsome, loud-roaring lion
45   in the bow of the ship and then amidships
a shaggy bear he caused to appear as a portent.
The bear reared with fury and the lion scowled dreadfully
on the topmost bench. The crew hastened in fear to the stern
and stood dumbfounded round the helmsman,
50   a man of prudent mind, as the lion swiftly lunged
at the captain and seized him. When they saw this,
they escaped evil fate by jumping overboard into the shining sea
and turning into dolphins. But, pitying the helmsman,
the god held him back and made him most happy with these words:
55   "Courage!...you are dear to my heart.
I am loud-roaring Dionysos, born of the daughter of Kadmos,
Semele, who found love in the arms of Zeus."
Hail, lovely-faced child of Semele! There is no way
one can forget you and still compose sweet songs.

8 : To Ares

Mighty Ares, golden-helmeted rider of chariots,
stout-hearted, shield-carrying, bronze-geared savior of cities,
strong-handed, unwearying lord of the spear, bulwark of Olympos,
father of fair Victory, helper of Themis.
5   You curb the unruly and lead truly just men,
O paragon of manly excellence, wheeling your luminous orb

through the seven-pathed constellations of the sky, where flaming
steeds ever carry you above the third heavenly arch.
Hearken, supporter of mortals and giver of flourishing youth,
10   and from above shine a gentle light on my life
and my martial prowess, that I may be able
to ward off bitter cowardice from my head,
to bend wisely my soul's beguiling impulse,
and to restrain the sharp fury of my heart, whenever
15   it provokes me to enter chilling battle. But, O blessed one,
give me courage to stay within the secure laws of peace
and to escape the enemy's charge and a violent death.

9 : To Artemis

Sing, O Muse, of Artemis, sister of the Far-shooting lord,
arrow-pouring virgin, who was nurtured with Apollon.
She waters her horses by Meles with its tall rushes
and from there on her golden chariot through Smyrna courses
5   to Klaros, rich in vineyards, where Apollon of the silver bow
sits waiting for the Far-shooting arrow-pourer.
Farewell to you and all the goddesses! Delight in my song!
I shall start my song with you
and then shall go to another hymn.

10 : To Aphrodite

I shall sing of Kythereia, born on Cyprus,
who brings sweet gifts to mortals, and whose lovely face
ever smiles radiant with lambent beauty on it.
Hail, goddess and mistress of well-built Salamis
5   and of sea-laved Cyprus! Grant me enchanting song.
Now I will remember you and another song as well.

11 : To Athena

I begin to sing of Pallas Athena, defender of cities,
awe-inspiring goddess; she and Ares care for deeds of war,
cities being sacked and cries of battle;
she protects an army going to war and returning.
5   Hail, O goddess! Grant me good fortune and happiness.

12 : To Hera

Of golden-throned Hera I sing, born of Rhea,
queen of the gods, unexcelled in beauty,
sister and glorious wife of loud-thundering Zeus.
All the gods on lofty Olympos reverence her
5   and honor her together with Zeus who delights in thunder.

13 : To Demeter

Of Demeter, the lovely-haired and revered goddess,
and of her daughter, Persephone of sublime beauty, I begin to sing.
Hail, O goddess! Keep this city safe, and guide my song.

14 : To the Mother of the Gods

Sing to me, O Muse, clear-voiced daughter of great Zeus,
of the mother of all gods and of all mortals.
In the din of rattles and drums and in the sound of pipes
she delights. In the howl of wolves and the roar of glaring lions,
5   in resounding mountains and wooded glens she finds her joy.
Farewell! I invite you and all the goddesses to delight in my song.

15 : To Lion-Hearted Herakles

I shall sing of Zeus's son, Herakles, noblest of mortals,
born at Thebes, city of lovely dances,
of the union of Alkmene with Zeus, lord of dark clouds.
In the past he wandered endlessly over the boundless earth and sea
5   on missions ordered by lord Eurystheus;
his reckless deeds were many and many the ordeals he suffered.
But now he joyously dwells in his beautiful abode
on snowy Olympos with fair-ankled Hebe as his spouse.
Hail, O lord and son of Zeus! Grant me virtue and happiness.

16 : To Asklepios

I begin to sing of Asklepios, healer of diseases,
son of Apollon. Noble Koronis, daughter
of King Phlegyas gave birth to him on the plain of Dotion,
to be a great joy to men and to charm evil pains away.
5   So hail, O lord! My song is a prayer to you.

17 : To the Dioskouroi

Sing, O clear-voiced Muse, of Kastor and Polydeukes,
sons of Tyndareus, sired also by Zeus;
mighty Leda gave birth to them beneath the peaks of Taygetos.
She succumbed in secrecy to the passion of Zeus, lord of dark clouds.
5   Hail, Tyndaridai, riders of swift horses!

18 : To Hermes

I sing of Hermes, the Kyllenian Argeiphontes,
who is lord of Kyllene and of Arcadia rich in flocks of sheep.
This helpful messenger of the gods was born of the amorous union
of the bashful daughter of Atlas with Zeus.
5   She shunned the company of the blessed gods
and lived in a thick-shaded cave. There, Kronion
lay with the fair-tressed nymph in the dead of night,
while sweet sleep overcame white-armed Hera;
so he escaped the eyes of both gods and mortals.
10   Hail, son of Zeus and Maia!
I began with you, but I will now turn to another hymn.
Hail, Hermes, guide and giver of things graceful and good!

19 : To Pan

Sing to me, O Muse, of Hermes's dear child,
the goat-footed, two-horned, din-loving one, who roams
over wooded glades together with the dance-loving nymphs;
they tread on the tops of sheer cliffs,
5   calling upon Pan, the splendid-haired and unkempt
god of shepherds, to whose domain all the snowy hills
and mountain peaks and rocky paths belong.
He wanders all over through the thick brushwood,
now drawn to gently flowing streams,
10   now again making his way through to steep crags
and climbing to the topmost peak overlooking the flocks.
Many times he careers through chalk-white, lofty mountains
and many times he drives beasts onto jutting rocks
and, his keen eye fixed on them, he slays them. Then only at evening
15   he shouts as he returns from the hunt and on his pipes of reed
he gently plays sweet music. In song he could even outdo
that bird that sits among the leaves at flower-rich springtime

and, pouring forth its dirge, trills honey-voiced tunes.
With him at that time are the clear-voiced mountain nymphs,
20   dancing nimbly and singing at some dark spring,
as the echo moans about the mountain peaks.
The god glides now here, now there, and then to the middle of the dance,
his quick feet set the pace. On his back he wears
a bay lynx-skin as his heart delights in the shrill songs
25   in a soft meadow where the crocus and the fragrant hyacinth
blossom forth and entwine with the grass in fast embrace.
They sing of the blessed gods and of lofty Olympos
and, above all others, they tell of helpful Hermes,
how he is the swift messenger to all the gods
30   and how he came to the mother of flocks, Arcadia, abounding in springs,
where there is a sacred precinct for him as god of Kyllene.
There, though he was a god, he tended curly-fleeced sheep
for a mortal man, because there came upon him and grew strong
a melting desire to lie with the fair-tressed daughter of Dryops.
35   His was a festive wedding, and inside the house she bore
to Hermes a dear son, from birth monstrous to behold,
with goat's feet and two horns, boisterous and sweet-laughing.
His mother sprang up and fled; the nurse in turn left the child behind
because she was afraid when she saw his wild and well-bearded face.
40   Helpful Hermes quickly received him into his arms,
and in his divine heart the joy overflowed.
He wrapped the child in snug skins of mountain hares
and swiftly went to the abodes of the immortals.
Then he set him down beside Zeus and the other gods
45   and showed them his boy: all of them were delighted
in their hearts and Bacchic Dionysos above all others.
They called him Pan because he cheered the hearts of all.
So hail to you, O lord! I propitiate you with song.
Now I shall remember you and another song as well.

20 : To Hephaistos

Sing, O clear-voiced Muse, of Hephaistos famous for skill,
who along with gray-eyed Athena taught fine crafts
to men of this earth; indeed before that time
they used to live in mountain caves like wild beasts.
5   From Hephaistos, the famous craftsman,
they learned skills and easily for the full year
they lead a carefree existence in their own homes.
Be kind to me, Hephaistos; grant me virtue and happiness.

21 : To Apollon

Phoibos, of you even the crying swan sings to flapping wings
as it swoops down upon the bank of the eddying river
Peneios. And of you the sweet-singing bard ever sings
first and last to his high-pitched lyre.
5   I salute you, lord! I propitiate you with my song.

22 : To Poseidon

I begin to sing of Poseidon, the great god,
mover of the earth and of the barren deep,
the sea-god who is lord of Helikon and broad Aigai.
O Earth-shaker, twofold is your god-given prerogative,
5   to be a tamer of horses and a savior of ships.
Hail, Poseidon, black-maned holder of the earth!
Have a kindly heart, O blessed one, and come to the aid of sailors!

23 : To Zeus

I shall sing of Zeus, the best and the greatest of gods,
far-seeing, mighty, fulfiller of designs who confides
his tight-knit schemes to Themis as she sits leaning upon him.
Be kind to me, far-seeing Kronides, most sublime and most glorious!

24 : To Hestia

Hestia, you tend the sacred dwelling
of the Far-shooting lord, Apollon, at holy Pytho,
as from your tresses flowing oil ever drips down.
Come to this house! Come in gentle spirit
5   with resourceful Zeus and give grace to my song!

25 : To the Muses and Apollon

Let me begin with the Muses and Apollon and Zeus,
because it is through the Muses and Far-shooting Apollon
that inspiration comes to singers and lyre players on the earth,
while kings are from Zeus. Blessed is the man whom the Muses
5   love, for sweet speech flows from his mouth.
Hail, children of Zeus! Do honor my song!
I shall remember you and another song as well.

26 : To Dionysos

I now sing of boisterous Dionysos whose head is crowned with ivy,
the noble son of Zeus and glorious Semele.
The lovely-haired nymphs nurtured him and from his lordly father
took him to their bosoms to cuddle and nurse
5   in the dells of Nysa. He grew up by his father's will
inside a sweet-smelling cave as one of the immortals.
But after the goddesses brought him up with many songs,
covered with ivy and laurel he started
haunting the wooded glens. The nymphs followed him
10   and he led the way as the boundless forest echoed with din.
So hail to you and hail to the luxuriance of your grapes!
Grant that we joyously reach these seasons
and many more years that will follow them.

27 : To Artemis

I sing of Artemis of the golden shafts, the modest maiden
who loves the din of the hunt and shoots volleys of arrows at stags.
She is the twin sister of Apollon of the golden sword,
and through shady mountains and windy peaks
5   she delights in the chase as she stretches her golden bow
to shoot the bitter arrows. The crests of tall mountains
tremble, and the thick-shaded forest resounds
dreadfully with the cries of beasts, while the earth
and the deep teeming with fish shudder. Hers is a mighty heart,
10   and she roams all over destroying the brood of wild beasts.
But when the arrow-pouring goddess who spots the wild beasts
has taken her pleasure and delighted her mind, after slacking
the well-taut bow, she comes to the great house of her dear brother,
Phoibos Apollon, at the rich district of Delphoi,
15   to set up the beautiful dance of the Muses and the Graces.
There she hangs her resilient bow and her quiver
and, wearing her graceful jewelry, she leads them
into dance. Divine is the sound they utter
as they sing of how fair-ankled Leto gave birth to children,
20   who among the gods are by far the best in deed and counsel.
Hail, children of Zeus and lovely-haired Leto!
I shall remember you and another song as well.

28 : To Athena

I begin to sing of Pallas Athena, the glorious goddess,
gray-eyed, resourceful, of implacable heart.
This bashful maiden is a mighty defender of cities,
the Tritogeneia, to whom Zeus the counselor himself
5   gave birth from his noble head; awe at her golden, resplendent,
warlike armor lay hold of all the immortal
onlookers. Before Zeus the aegis-holder
she sprang swiftly from his immortal head,
brandishing a sharp-pointed spear. Great Olympos quaked
10   dreadfully under the might of the gray-eyed goddess, as the earth
all about resounded awesomely, and the sea moved
and heaved with purple waves. The briny swell calmed down
when the splendid son of Hyperion stopped
his fleet-footed horses long enough for maidenly
15   Pallas Athena to take the divine weapons
off her shoulders as Zeus the counselor exulted.
Hail to you, child of aegis-holding Zeus!
I shall remember you and another song as well.

29 : To Hestia

Hestia, in the lofty dwellings of all,
both of immortal gods and of all the men who walk the earth,
you have attained an eternal abode and you have the place of honor,
together with a fair and honorific prize: for without you
5   there can be no feasts for mortals, if the man in charge does not
pour sweet wine to you first, and then again last at the end.
And you, Argeiphontes, son of Zeus and Maia,
messenger of the blessed gods, golden-staffed giver of blessings,
dwell with Hestia in beautiful houses, with loving hearts

. . . .
10   I ask you and revered and dear Hestia for help.
Since both of you know the good works of the people
of this earth, be their watchful and youthful companions!
Hail, O daughter of Kronos, both you and Hermes of the golden wand!
I shall remember you and another song as well.

30 : To Earth, Mother of All

I shall sing of Earth and its firm foundations, mother of all,
oldest of all, who nourishes all things living on land.

Her beauty nurtures all creatures that walk upon the land,
and all that move in the deep or fly in the air.
5   From you come beautiful children and lovely fruitbearing trees.
O mighty one, yours is the power to grant life or take it away from
mortals. Blessed is the man you favor
with willing heart, for he will have everything in abundance.
His life-giving land teems with crops, and on his fields
10   his flocks thrive while his house is filled with goods.
Such men with just laws rule a city of lovely women,
while much prosperity and wealth attend them.
Their sons glory in youthful glee
and their daughters with cheerful hearts, wreathed with flowers
15   play and frisk over the flowery meadows of the field.
These are the ones you honor, O revered goddess of plenty!
Hail, mother of the gods and wife of starry Ouranos!
For my song do grant me livelihood that gladdens the heart,
and I shall remember you and another song as well.

31 : To Helios

O Muse Kalliope, begin to sing again
of brilliant Helios whom cow-eyed Euryphaëssa
bore to the son of Gaia and starry Ouranos.
Hyperion married his own sister, the glorious
5   Euryphaëssa, who bore him beautiful children:
rosy-armed Eos, fair-tressed Selene,
and tireless Helios, so much like the immortals;
he shines his light on both mortals and immortals
as he rides his horses. His eyes gaze fiercely
10   from his golden helmet, while his luminous rays
sparkle brilliantly and the shining cheek-pieces
descend from his head over his temples and border his graceful
and effulgent face. On his body a beautiful and finely woven
garment shimmers as the winds blow, and his stallions

. . . .

15   After he stays his golden-yoked chariot and horses there,
he wondrously sends them to the ocean through the sky.
Hail, O lord! Kindly grant me livelihood that cheers the heart.
Starting with you I shall glorify the race of mortal men,
the demigods whose deeds the gods have revealed to men.

32 : To Selene

Muses, sweet-speaking daughters of Zeus son of Kronos,
mistresses of song, sing next of long-winged Moon!
From her immortal head a heaven-sent glow
envelops the earth and great beauty arises
5   under its radiance. From her golden crown the dim air
is made to glitter as her rays turn night to noon.
Bright Selene bathes her beautiful body
in the Ocean, puts on her splendid clothes,
and harnesses her proud-necked and glistening steeds;
10   she drives them on swiftly as their manes play
with the evening light, dividing the months. Her great orbit is full
and as she waxes a most brilliant light appears
in the sky. So to mortals she is a sign and a token.
Once the son of Kronos shared her bed and her love;
15   she became pregnant and gave birth to Pandeia,
a maiden outstanding for beauty among the immortal gods.
Hail, queen and white-armed goddess, splendid Selene,
kindly and fair-tressed! Beginning with you I shall sing
of the glories of demigods, whose deeds are ennobled by bards,
20   who serve the Muses with their skill in song.

33 : To the Dioskouroi

Quick-glancing Muses, sing of Zeus's sons,
the Tyndaridai, splendid children of fair-ankled Leda,
horse-taming Kastor, and blameless Polydeukes.
She found love in the arms of Kronion, lord of dark clouds,
5   under the peak of Taygetos, that lofty mountain,
and gave birth to these children as saviors of mortals on this earth
and on swift-sailing ships, whenever wintry storms
sweep along the pitiless sea. Then men go
to the edge of the stern and with offers of white lambs
10   they pray and call upon the sons of great Zeus.
When gusty winds and the waves of the sea
bring the ship under water, they suddenly appear,
having sped through the air with rushing wings,
and at once they calm the cruel windy storms
15   and level the waves of the foaming high seas.
These are fair signs of a reward for their labors
and when they see them, they rejoice and they quit their toilsome struggle.

Hail, Tyndaridai, riders of swift horses!
I shall remember you and another song as well.

To Guest-Friends

Have respect for him who has a need of gifts and of shelter,
all you who dwell in the lofty city of Hera, the lovely-faced nymph,
at the foot of towering Saidene,
drinking the divine water of the fair-flowing river,
5   the tawny Hermos, whom immortal Zeus sired.

NOTES

1 : Fragments of the Hymn to Dionysos

The hymn we have before us now consists of two fragments. We cannot be absolutely sure that these two fragments are part of the same hymn. The title *Eiraphiotes,* which occurs in both fragments, is a positive but hardly adequate indication. On the other hand, it is difficult to find one peremptory argument proving that our two fragments do not belong to the same hymn. The first nine lines are quoted by Diodorus Siculus (3.66.3). Lines 10–21 are found on folium 31 of codex *M.* The date of composition must be early; eighth to sixth centuries BC is a good guess. Diodorus attributed it to Homer, and this is some indication of an early date. Lines 10–21 are definitely the conclusion to a longer hymn. These lines are found in such a position in *M*—a whole quire and a leaf just before folium 31 are missing—that our fragment might well have belonged to a hymn that was four hundred to six hundred lines long. The beginning lines of the hymn perhaps belonged to a performance of athletic games.

1. Eiraphiotes: The ancients puzzled over the meaning and etymology of this word. One of their explanations—and incidentally the one that prevailed in their minds—connects the word with "rhaptô" ("to sew") and alludes to the traditional version of the myth according to which Zeus rescued the yet unborn child from the ashes of his burnt mother and *sewed him into* his thigh. Drakanon, at the end of this line, is most likely a promontory jutting out from the coast of the island of Kos.

2. Ikaros must be a small island near Samos. We cannot be entirely sure which island this is. Most likely, it is Ikaria. According to mythology, Ikaros, son of Daedalus, fell into the sea somewhere near this island or perhaps on it. Daedalus was the famous architect who built the labyrinth for King Minos of Crete. Naxos, at the end of this line, is one of the Cycladic islands.

4. The traditional account gives Thebes as the birthplace of Dionysos and Semele as his mother; another mythological tradition makes him the offspring of an incestuous union between Zeus and his own daughter, Persephone.

8. Nysa: This is such a frequent toponym, found as far as India, that it would be unwise to be dogmatic about its precise location. The author of this hymn obviously accepts the theory that the name of the god is derived from the name of his father (*Zeus,* gen. *Dios*) and the name of his birthplace, which he places somewhere near Egypt.

11. Codex *M* contains an incomprehensible reading here. I have translated Allen's emendation in his 1983 edition of the hymns, for lack of something more convincing. That the dismemberment of Dionysos as Zagreus may be alluded to here is an attractive hypothesis, but since the Titans dismembered Dionysos, I fail to see why we should have "he cut (you)." The triennial festivals (*trietêrides*) of our line would be celebrated on alternate years according to our way of reckoning.

17. Whoever has read the *Bacchae* of Euripides would easily agree that *gynaimanês* (woman-maddener) is a very apt epithet for Dionysos.

21. Here Thyône is another name for Semele. In some sources, she is a nurse of Dionysos, and in others she is given as his mother with no implication that this is an alternative name.

2 : To Demeter

The earliest mention of Zeus's union with Demeter and of the rape of Persephone by Hades is found in Hesiod's *Theogony* 912–14. The *Iliad* and the *Odyssey* ignore the story, but this is no proof that Homer did not know about it. It is possible that its purely chthonic character may have struck him as incongruous with the Olympic pantheon that dominates his epics. Of the subsequent treatments of the subject—and there were many—I should like to mention Euripides's *Helena* 1301–68; Kallimachos's *Hymn to Demeter* 6; and Ovid's *Fasti* 4.419–616, and *Metamorphoses* 5.385–661. The date of the hymn cannot be fixed with precision. Both archaeological evidence from the site of Eleusis and internal evidence from the hymn point to a date that cannot be later than the end of the seventh century. The Hall of Rites (*telestêrion*), which must have been built when Eleusis came under Athenian control sometime at the very end of the seventh century, is not mentioned in the hymn. This rather powerful argument establishes the end of the seventh century as a *terminus ante quem* for the composition of the hymn. The terrace structure, now referred to as *temenos,* seems to have been built in the eighth century. However, it is not this structure but rather the one de-scribed as Megaron B—situated on the east slope of the citadel of Eleusis—that must be the temple referred to in the *Hymn to Deme-ter* 2.270–74. It was discovered by Kourou-niotes in the excavation of 1931 and 1932, and it dates back to Mycenaean times, fifteenth to thirteenth centuries BC. The *Marmor Parium* places the advent of Demeter to Eleusis in the fifteenth century. Greek tradi-tion held that Eumolpos, the founder of the powerful sacerdotal order of the Eumolpids, was a contemporary of Erechtheus, who also belongs to the fifteenth century. The *Marmor Parium* is a piece of Athenian propaganda. Early involvement of Athens in significant events is not to be trusted.

Aristotle has preserved for us the tradi-tion that the *Eleusinia* were instituted c. 1300 BC. All this points to an early Mycenaean origin of Demeter's cult at Eleusis. (For the identification of Megaron B with the temple of the hymn, see Mylonas [1972, 33–49].) However, this evidence does not help us establish a *terminus post quem* for the composition of the hymn. It is certainly much later in time than the tradition that it preserves. More helpful in dating it is the absence of any reference to Athens.

Since Eleusis came under Athenian control sometime in the second half of the seventh century, it may have been composed in the first half of the seventh century. The absence of any reference to Athens speaks not only for this earlier date but also for an Eleusinian rhapsode as the author.

The *Hymn to Demeter* is above all a record of poetic fundamentals. However, it has been studied more for what it can tell us about the Eleusinian mysteries and less for its poetic beauty. Since the initiates to the mysteries were sworn to secrecy with regard to the rituals that took place inside the *telestêrion,* it is small wonder that we know next to nothing about these rituals. The telltale accounts of early Christian zealots are not worthless, but we must not forget that they are biased polemics. Yet, the hymn yields valuable information not only about the preparation for initiation and the significance of the ritualistic regimen but also about the very nature of Demeter's cult at Eleusis. Thus the hymn leaves no doubt that whatever went on at Eleusis dealt with the mystery of life and regeneration as well as with the impenetrable secret of death and the hope for some ray of light in the tene-brous underworld. Furthermore, the hymn teaches us that the cult was chthonic, most likely pre-Hellenic in origin and indigenous to Eleusis. By this I do not mean that similar cults did not exist elsewhere. Far from it. I mean only that the Eleusinian version of what is in essence a human universal and a religious archetype had its own distinct identity, which need not have been import-ed from somewhere else. As Jane Harrison aptly put it, "Demeter at Eleusis did not borrow her cymbals from Rhea, she had her own" (1991, 561).

The site of Eleusis and all the area around it, including the Thriasion field, have been heavily damaged by industrial development. Driving through the place evokes visions of hell. An effort is being made now to rectify this sad situation. Eleusis is chosen by the European Union to be cultural capital of Europe for the year 2021.

The great goddess has not vanished from the face of Greece. In Paroikia, Paros, the cathedral of Panagia Ekatopyliani (Panagia of the Hundred Gates) lies on top of an ancient temple of Demeter. Throughout the Hellenic world, Panagia is the epithet that refers to the All-Holy Mother of Jesus. Through an aperture in the church floor, one may see a couple of the pillars of the ancient temple. On top of the hill at Eleusis, a very interesting small chapel greets the visitor. This chapel is dedicated to Panagia Mesosporitissa (Panagia of the Middle of the Sowing Season). The presentation of the Virgin Mary in the temple of Jerusalem is celebrated on November 21. Ancient and later Christian traditions blend on this day. In other parts of Greece, Panagia is celebrated as Polysporitissa (Panagia of the Abundance of Seeds). Farming families boil cereal grains and eat them in a sort of a Thanksgiving meal and a prayerful reminder of Virgin Mary's benevolence. In Greece this time of the year calls for fall plowing and fall planting. This special meal of cereal grains is intended to promote fertility.

In the *Hymn to Demeter* we have the splicing of two profound motifs of Greek culture, marriage and death. The marriage of Persephone to Hades symbolized by the pomegranate is, at the same time, her death. These two motifs have survived to this day in wedding songs that are sung when the bride leaves the home of her family to an unknown future. The theme has been explored by Georgios Giannakis (1998).

3. "Gave" is both appropriate and consistent with Zeus's position as "father of gods and men." Of course, "gave" here almost means "permitted" or "allowed," but the notion of giving Persephone away as a bride is also inherent. Hesiod expresses the same idea in *Theogony* 914. Later versions of the story, which make Zeus act under the constraint of Fate or have Hades fall victim to the designs of a capricious Aphrodite, must be the result of learned mythographic speculation or of poetic fancy.

4. Scholars have not been able to determine the propriety or significance of the adjective that I am translating as "of the golden sword." Lycophron mentions an obscure cult of the sword-bearing Demeter in Boeotia, and it is possible that this cult was a survival from an earlier, more widespread, aspect of the cult of Demeter.

5–14. The flower gathering activity by Perse-phone and the daughters of Okeanos is an icon of youth and innocence, which sometimes comes with unforeseeable dangers. Until quite recently in Greece, boys and girls in elementary schools gathered flowers on Good Friday and helped decorate the Epitaphios (Tomb of Christ). It is interesting that, although other flowers are present in the poem, the narcissus is given the prominence that it doubtless deserved as a flower especially connected with the Great Goddesses (see Sophocles *Oedipus Coloneus* 683). The chthonic nature of this flower is evident in its being sacred to the Eumenides, and Artemidoros tells us that it was also funereal (*Oneirokritikos* 1.77). The association of the narcissus with death could be attributed both to its real or presumed soporific qualities and to the fact that in myth it was the lure that led to the rape of Persephone and her sojourn in Hades for one-third of the year during which nature "died."

15–21. Persephone is violently abducted, taken away, not only from her mother and her home but from the entire upperworld. The abduction is paradoxical. Why does Hades need a wife? Certainly not for having children. However, Hades can use Persephone to gain a foothold in the upperworld. Inherent in the whole idea of abduction is the idea of death. In the underworld, Persephone is a *xêne* (stranger). Until recently when a young woman left her home to become someone's bride, her friends, usually young women of her age, sang heart-rending songs. Such songs are almost always anonymous. Here is an example:

> Mother do not scold me, I am leaving
> now
> to go away from home.
> When you come to our church,
> you will not find my spot—it shall be
> empty.

Folk songs from the Agrafa Mountains mention a meadow, a widowed mother, and an orphaned daughter. In such songs, the daughter wears very dark colors:

> The meadows are greening
> and tears come to my eyes
> for a widow's daughter,
> who wears very dark colors.

17. Scholarly efforts to identify the Nysian field have not yielded any credible results.

23. We should not be surprised that a Mediterranean poet chose to endow the olive trees with the ability to hear. The Greeks, ancient and modern, frequently grant human attributes not only to animals but also to mountains, trees, and the like. One of the earliest instances is to be found in *Iliad* 3.275–80.

24. This is one of the earliest references to Hekate, who is the daughter of the Titan Persês (so spelled in other sources) and Asteriê (see Hesiod *Theogony* 411). The fact that she is not mentioned in Homer testifies not only to a relatively late arrival in Greece, most likely from the East, but also to a date of composition later than that of the two great Homeric epics.

Hekate was exclusively a women's goddess. Indeed women, usually in the evening, gathered at her shrines, which frequently were erected at *trivia*, places where three roads intersected. Hekate was associated with magical, frequently malevolent practices. She was connected with the waning and waxing of the moon. Hesiod's *Theogony* presents Hekate as a compassionate and generous goddess who has jurisdiction in the sky, the earth, and the underworld (lines 404ff.). Clearly, as he frequently does with other aspects of religion, Hesiod is trying to integrate Hekate into the more civilized domain of Greek religion.

30–32. Hades comes on a chariot. We are not told anything about his face or his body. He is more like a phantom, a dark power of the endless abyss. No desire for Persephone is expressed, no compliment is granted, and there is no attempt to lure Persephone with words of love. This violent groom does not come with gifts. After all, he is a taker, and not a giver, at all times.

42. It is odd that Demeter wears a dark veil, a sign of mourning, even before she hears of her daughter's abduction. We may be faced with a case in which later ritual influences mythopoetic composition. Even in later Greek culture, the dark clothing signifies grief over the death of a loved one. Many widowed women wear black after the death of their husbands for the rest of their lives. From the earliest times, the word "black" or "dark," especially when applied to clothing, had mostly negative associations. Up to our times, in some of the dirges the earth is frequently called "black earth." For a thorough study of the ritualistic conventions of the Greek lament, see Alexiou (2002).

In *Iliad* 2.834, death itself is black. Pain can be black as in *Iliad* 4.117. Ominous and threatening anger is described as black in *Iliad* 1.103. For gestures that express extreme grief, see *Iliad* 19.283–300. In this passage, Briseis tears the soft skin of her neck and of her beautiful face to show extreme grief over the death of Patroklos. Demeter does not go to such extremes. During her wandering all over the earth for nine days and nine nights, she abstains from eating ambrosia and from drinking nectar. Persephone may be abducted but, being the daughter of Zeus and Demeter, she is immortal. So then, Demeter is mourning because her daughter is taken away by force.

47. The number of days may indeed be conventional. But, although we do not know the exact duration of the fast, either at the Eleusinian mysteries or at the Thesmophoria, we do know that the period of strict mourning after someone's death as well as certain expiatory rites lasted for nine days. Three and its multiples were frequently employed then as even now. Thus, the Graces were three, the Muses nine, the Olympian gods twelve, and so on. Greek culture has been very conservative when it comes to matters concerning death. The nine-day period following someone's death is marked by a memorial service that is almost a repetition of the funeral. When Apollon attacks the Achaean camp with his pestiferous arrows, he does so for nine whole days (*Iliad* I.53). Dêô, most likely a diminutive, is another name for Demeter.

48. In the myth, Demeter holds torches in her hands because she is searching even in dark caves and wooded glens in which the abductor might have sought refuge. In the ritual of the Eleusinian mysteries and the Thesmophoria, the torches may have been symbols of the solar light and warmth that must triumph over the infernal cold darkness of the winter so that nature may come alive again in the spring.

49–50. These tokens of extreme grief are not substantially different from those practiced by the Greeks of today during the Holy Week and especially on Good Friday. Devout Christians follow a certain dietary regimen and abstain from all festive activities during Holy Week. On Saturday preceding Easter Sunday, as close to midnight as possible, there is a light-giving ceremony, and, after the conclusion of the liturgy, participants carry the light of the Resurrection to their homes (see *Iliad* 23.43–48).

52. The author of this hymn definitely identifies Hekate with the moon. The torch must be symbolic of the lunar light emanating from Hekate, the moon-goddess.

62. The sun does see everything, and so he watches gods and men. Similarly, the moon sees all and it is no accident that the cry of Persephone does not escape the attention of either Helios or Hekate. The idea of the all-seeing sun is commonplace in Greek poetry down to the present day. Thus Homer's "O sun, you who see and hear all things" (*Iliad* 3.277) is reechoed by Kazantzakis (1985) in "Great sun, who pass on high yet watch all things below."

74. "Hyperionidês" ("the son of Hyperion") is a patronymic; the usual form is "Hyperion" as in *Odyssey* 1.8 (see also *Hymn to Apollon* 3.369).

96. Keleos, his wife Metaneira, and even his daughters were still revered at Eleusis in classical times (see Paus. 1.39).

99. The Parthenion well has not been convincingly identified with any modern landmark. In ancient times, it came to be confused with another well, the Kallichoron, which was near the precinct of Eleusis. For details, see Mylonas (1972, 46–47, 150).

101. Disguises in order to conceal true identity are in keeping with the conventions of the Greek epic. Aphrodite appears to Helen in the guise of an old woman (*Iliad* 3.386–89) and to Anchises as a young Phrygian maiden (*Hymn to Aphrodite*, 5.81–83, 5.107–42).

109–10. On the authority of Pamphos, Pausanias names only three princesses, daughters of Keleos: Diogeneia, Pammerope, and Saisara. See also Commentary by Allen, Halliday, and Sikes (1936).

122. Dôs (giving) is not an unlikely pseudonym for Demeter. The word occurs in Hesiod *Works and Days* 356 and is equivalent to "*dosis*" ("giving"). The goddess is playful because, on the one hand, she does not give her true name, but on the other hand, she gives a name that is highly suggestive of Demeter's nature as a generous and "giving" divinity.

123. Some have tried to discover the origin of the Eleusinian cult in this story. But the story of a young girl kidnapped by Cretan pirates may be no more than a convenient lie. Odysseus pretends that he is a Cretan on three different occasions (*Odyssey* 13.256; 14.199; 19.172).

126. Thorikos was north of cape Sounion (see "Sunium" in *The Oxford Classical Dictionary* [Hornblower, Spawforth, and Eidinow 2012]).

135–40. Demeter at the well is a very significant icon. The well is a source of water and therefore a source of life. The four daughters of the local king come to the well to fetch water. Demeter, at this point just a shriveled-up crone, asks the girls to find her work and shelter with one of the noble local families. To her request she attaches a solemn wish: "May you find good husbands and may you have children." The wish is still heard in Greece, especially in the countryside.

153. In classical times, Triptolemos became a very important figure in the Eleusinian mysteries. Here he is merely another one of the local princes, a fact that testifies to the great antiquity of the hymn. His parentage is uncertain, but for Apollodoros he is the eldest son of Keleos and Metaneira (*Bibliotheca* 1.5.2). Dioklos may be the same as the Megarian hero Dioklês, and his inclusion here may not be unrelated to the dependence of Eleusis on Megara in earlier times.

154–55. Although some later sources make Dioklos the son of Triptolemos, Polyxeinos, Eumolpos, and Dolichos are otherwise unknown.

174–83. The hymn is pervaded with the beauty and power of the feminine, a power that is archetypal. The four daughters of Keleos, king of Eleusis, have good news for the grieving goddess. They run like deer or calves on a meadow. This meadow underscores their grace. As they run, their crocus-colored hair tosses about their shoulders. Their youth contrasts with the age of the stranger. When she follows them to the palace, there are five women heading to a common purpose. Once they all are inside the palace, two more women, Queen Metaneira and Iambê, her servant, complete the group. Demeter's refusal to accept all offers of hospitality seems to be born of feminine anger.

187. The queen with the baby on her lap invites comparisons with similar iconic mothers in various religions. Familiar to most readers is the image of the Virgin Mary holding the baby Jesus. Her presence in Greece is very strong. She is addressed by about five hundred worshipful epithets.

188–89. Demeter's head touches the roof much as Aphrodite's does in the *Hymn to Aphrodite* 5.173–74. The Greeks generally ascribed superhuman stature to the gods (see *Iliad* 4.443). Radiance as a token of divine presence (see *Hymn to Apollon* 3.444–45) has found ready acceptance in Christian accounts of miraculous epiphany. See the notes on lines 275–80.

188–91. The extraordinary size of the goddess in her assertive epiphany manifests her divinity. Demeter fills the place with divine light. The radiance is distinctly feminine. It is not invasive. It is soft and gentle, more like moonlight. Later in the hymn, the goddess has reason to be angry at the queen. In that case, her anger becomes manifest in the image of a flash of lightning (275–80). In the *Hymn to Aphrodite*, a lunar radiance emanates from the breasts of the goddess (5.84–90). A similar radiance also emanates from her beautiful cheeks (5.174).

191–205. This charming and intriguing incident in the story of Demeter's search for Persephone is still awaiting the day on which some incisive mind will shed light on its origin and implications. On the surface, the story is simple: Demeter is deeply distraught and a funny old lady entertains her with some coarse jokes and makes her laugh. But who is Iambê, and why in the Orphic version it is not Iambê but the Eleusinian queen, Baubô, who induces the goddess to forget her sorrow and laugh by lifting her robe and exposing her pudenda? From ancient sources we know that at nearly every festival in honor of Demeter, including the procession to Eleusis (cf. Arist. *Frogs* 372ff.), there was frivolity in the

form of obscene gestures. We have reason to believe that these gestures were sexual in character and thus a most appropriate part of a fertility cult. For the Orphic version of the story, see Kern (1922, frag. 46–53, especially frag. 52).

Lines 191–205 have preserved the elements of a ritual drama of initiation. A mother's grief over the abduction of her virgin daughter by a violent and infernal stranger is assuaged by humorous crudities and by emotional and social accommodations made to necessity and natural law. Reconciliation is at the center of the efforts of all involved. Young women learned from older women, such as the goddess, the queen, and the wise old Iambê. Within the context of a significant ritual, three actresses teach matters profound and intimate to an audience of four young maidens. The speechless infant stands for the ultimate reality that is integral to the propagation of life. Some of the names associated with Demeter's arrival at Eleusis and her visit to the palace of the local king suggest that music was an important part of mystical rites in honor of the goddess since very primitive times. Iambê is certainly connected with "iambos" and "iamb," and Keleos, the name of the king of Eleusis, might easily refer to a percussion instrument such as a drumstick. In the Orphic version mentioned above, the sound of the queen's name, Baubô, prompts the imagination to suspect that an echomimetic syllable was reduplicated in imitation of a loud and deep sound. Her husband's name, Dysaulês, and "aulos" ("flute") clearly have something in common. Then there is Eumolpos (good singer) of line 154. Perhaps in primeval times the grain used to prepare a drink for a profoundly significant fertility ritual was crushed by means of pestle and mortar in such a way as to produce a simple iambic rhythm. Some of the implements used as musical instruments may have been personified.

206–11. The potion the goddess orders consists of barley—most likely cracked barley—water, and pennyroyal, a variety of mint. Barley seed stands for seed in general while mint suggests a feminine additive, perhaps to promote feminine fertility. Water, at all times, signifies the source of

life. This potion contains similarities to
kollyba, the wheaten trays offered to the
dead, usually at the graveside. Both ancient
and modern *kollyba* are made with boiled
wheat to which pomegranate seeds are
added. It is possible that Demeter asks for
such a preparation because she is mourning
for her daughter who might be dead. The
emphasis is on the idea that until she finds
Persephone she is in a state of mourning.

207–8. It should be mentioned here that most
sacrifices to Demeter and to many other
chthonic gods were wineless. The reason
for this taboo remains unknown.

208–10. The Greek word for this potion is
"kykeôn" (literally, "a mixed or stirred
drink"). On the authority of Clement of
Alexandria, we know that a mixture of water, mint (pennyroyal), and flour was used
as a drink of initiation into the Eleusinian
mysteries. However, this act of initiation
must not have been part of the secret and
ineffable rites performed at the *telesterion*
(hall of rituals) because depictions of it are
found on Attic vases.

225–30. Demeter becomes a surrogate mother
to infant Demophoön. The goddess
adopted a child that would take the place
of Persephone, her lost daughter. To match
the difference between divine and human
status, she took care to raise Demophoön
in ways that would make him a god. She
fed him ambrosia. In the darkness of night,
she stuck him into the fire like a firebrand.
The purpose of this second action was to
eradicate his mortal elements, to purify
him of them. In a way, the immersion of a
Christian child into baptismal water, which
is the practice in the Orthodox Church, has
the same purpose. The baptized human
being dies in the water and is resurrected as
a new person when taken out of the water
(see Saint Paul's *Epistle to the Romans*, Rom
6:1–5).

228–30. In "the Undercutter" and "the tree-felling creature," scholars have, I think rightly,
seen references to the belief that toothache
is caused by a certain worm. The goddess
wisely refers to it with a periphrasis for fear
that calling it by its name might provoke its
instant appearance.

231–41. Parallels to the story of the child
are found not only in Greek literature

but also in the legends of other nations
(we have an analogue in the story of Isis
and the infant son of the king of Byblos
in Plutarch's *Isis and Osiris* 16). In Greek
literature, the story of Thetis and Achilles
shows that the motif is not confined to this
hymn. Apollodoros and other later writers
depart from the tradition of this hymn and,
accommodating the eventual prominence
of Triptolemos in the Eleusinian mysteries,
tell us either that Demophoön died when
Demeter's strange doings were discovered
by Metaneira (Apollodoros *Bibliotheca*
1.5.1) or that the child nursed by Demeter
was not Demophoön but Triptolemos
(see among others, Ovid *Metamorphoses*
5.645; Nicander *Thêriaka* 484). As Demeter
herself explains in lines 260–61, the purpose
of anointing Demophoön with ambrosia
and hiding him in the fire by night was to
make him immortal. The reader may recall
that Thetis put drops of ambrosia into the
nose of Patroklos to prevent decay of his
body (*Iliad* 19.39). According to Lycophron
(*Cassandra* 178ff.), Thetis immortalized
six of her children by burning away their
mortal parts in the fire. Her attempt to make
Achilles immortal by placing him on the
fire and then anointing him with ambrosia
was frustrated by Peleus, who intervened
just when the goddess had subjected all but
the anklebone of the child to this treatment
(Apollodoros 3.13.6). It is interesting that
fire and ambrosia are used both in the case
of Achilles and Demophoön. As Apollodoros tells the story, Thetis hid Achilles
in the fire by night and anointed him with
ambrosia by day. Although in the story of
Demophoön it is not clear what procedure
is followed, the treatment with fire took
place at night, the implication thereby being
that the anointing occurred during the day.
Perhaps the origin of using fire and then
ambrosia to make someone immortal may
not be unconnected with the technique of
the smith, who first "hides" the metal in fire
and then dips it in water to harden it.

245–95. Thetis dips the infant Achilles into the
water of the Styx to make him immortal.
This mythic river encircles the underworld.
The gods swear by it in a test of truth. If
they lie, they are punished (see Hesiod
Theogony 792–806).

265–67. We know of no civil war at Eleusis, and this may indeed be an *ex post facto* prophecy, in which case, given the antiquity of the hymn, we may be dealing with a facet of Eleusinian history antedating the prominence that Eleusis gained as a result of the cult of Demeter.

270–72. For the identification of the temple mentioned in these lines, see Mylonas (1972, 34ff.). This book remains an authoritative source of information on the archaeological site of Eleusis and on the Homeric *Hymn to Demeter* (see especially Mylonas 1972, 224–285). In 1892 a well was discovered on the site. This well may not be properly identified as the Parthenion or Kallichoron well of the *Hymn to Demeter*. It may indeed be a well inspired by the hymn, a devotional structure of classical or post-classical, indeed even Roman, times.

275–80. These lines present us with a fuller and more dramatic epiphany of the goddess. Earlier the manifestation of divine presence was accompanied by supernatural size and the wondrous radiance that filled the doorway (188–89). The light of the second epiphany is like that of lightning and fills the entire mansion. The mood signified by this light is aggressive, invasive, and perhaps also less feminine. Demeter rids herself of all signs of old age. Beauty is now wafted all about her. She is enveloped by a lovely fragrance. Her blond hair cascades down her shoulders. The whole place is filled with light. The child's mother is speechless. His four sisters offer comfort to the baby. They hug and bathe him.

  In the tradition of the Greek Orthodox Church, the foundation of many churches is connected with the persistent appearance of a light during the night. Divine fragrance is also a testimony of sanctity. A good example is found in the story of Saint Demetrios, patron saint of Thessaloniki, the second largest city of Greece. The epithet Myrovlitis ("myrrh-exuding") is attributed to him as part of his holiness.

292. Keleos, the child's father, knows nothing as yet. This nocturnal propitiation of the goddess is attended solely by women and may correspond to the *pannychis,* the all-night women's festival of the Thesmophoria.

302. *"Xanthos"* ("blond") must be used as conventionally here as elsewhere in Greek epic (see 279).

305–13. It has not been determined whether these lines conceal a reference to lean years of famine and destitution for the Eleusinians, destitution that they were known to have once suffered. Demeter does not propose to scale Olympos. She does not use violent language against the gods. She also refrains from aggressive physical action against mortals. She punishes by depriving others of her benevolent presence. It could be said that she exercises her powers in a distinctly feminine way.

324–33. All the gods visit Demeter at Eleusis with gifts. They beg her to relent her anger. However, no one can persuade her to let go of her emotional fury.

334–46. Zeus sends Hermes to the underworld to ask Hades to return Persephone to her mother. Hermes finds Hades sitting on his bed with Persephone next to him. The image is entirely conjugal.

345–56. Hermes takes the message to Hades. Demeter, in a state of dreadful wrath, stays away from the company of the gods. She secludes herself inside her temple at Eleusis. Hermes acts only as a messenger. He must execute his mission. He is entirely unemotional.

349. "Erebos" here means "darkness."

357–69. Hades's smile indicates that he has played well. By having Persephone share his bed, he has a lien on her. The pomegranate is a symbol of fertility. The seeds, red and flesh-colored, are covered by the womblike rind. Yet, there can be no fertility in the underworld, which is motionless and hopeless. The domain of Hades is an enormous jail, a death camp. There are neither feelings nor flowers in this wedding. In fact, there is no wedding. It is obvious that Hades is trying to renegotiate the terms of the tripartite cosmic order. Within the new order, which includes Persephone as queen of the underworld part of the year, Hades settles for a compromise. He is no longer absolute master of the underworld, especially when Persephone is with him.

358. Modern Greeks signal "no" by swiftly raising their eyebrows. Knitted or arched eyebrows may indicate mood. Thus,

"smiling brows" may be a reference to an especially Greek facial expression or merely a hyperbole for "he really smiled."

370–76. Persephone is happy. Her infernal husband gives her a grain of pomegranate to eat. This detail is significant. It is an allegory for sexual union. It means that no matter what Persephone does, she will be bonded to Hades because she has slept with him.

372–74. Apollodoros follows the hymn closely with respect to line 372 (cf. 1.5.3). In Ovid *Metamorphoses* 5.535, Persephone is not given the fruit by the god of the underworld, but she finds it in a garden and eats seven seeds. Some obscure numerological allusion may be hidden in this version. The pomegranate was widely used in both ritual and folk medicine, but our poet may have chosen it rather than some other fruit because the plant had definite chthonic connections. The tree was thought to have sprung from the blood of Dionysos Zagreus (Clement of Alexandria *Protreptikos* 2.19), and pomegranate seeds are still used by Greeks in the *kollyba,* the wheat offerings distributed to the congregation in memorial services in honor of the dead. By eating a fruit that is especially connected with the world of the dead and by accepting what is a gift from the ruler of that world, Persephone establishes a *xenia,* a guest-host tie that comes with an obligation for her both to go back and to give in return.

375–83. Hades rides his chariot. Persephone obviously sits next to him. The chariot is drawn by immortal horses. The phrase "immortal horses" clashes with the scene, which lies entirely in the realm of death. But "immortal" here may be simply a formulaic attribute. The landscape of Hades is a joyless one. Even the departure of Persephone from Hades is an almost mechanical affair. There is no farewell; there are no tears. Through sea and mountain, they come to Demeter's temple at Eleusis. Persephone leaps to her mother's embrace.

393–94. Demeter asks Persephone what it is that she may have eaten in the underworld. Persephone reveals to her mother that Hades offered her a pomegranate seed. The symbolism here is a sexual one.

398–403. Persephone will be with her mother two-thirds of the year. She will spend one-third of it in the underworld. Greece does not have the severe winters of Northern Europe. The heart of the winter lasts for about three months: December, January, and February. The sojourn of Persephone in the underworld corresponds to the time that so many seeds lie dormant in the ground. Of the explanations given for Persephone's sojourn in Hades for one-third of the year, the ancient Stoic doctrine that this period stood for the time during which seeds are "hidden" in the ground is certainly both logical and plausible. Lines 387–400 have been restored. Therefore, everything pertaining to these lines is highly conjectural.

414–16. Zeus was in on the abduction plan. The divine patriarch may simply want to acquire some share of power in the lower world, as a sort of father-in-law of Hades. This arrangement was a practice by various dynasties that used matrimony for political alliances. Toward the end of the Byzantine Empire there were cases in which princesses of the ruling imperial house were married off to Muslim rulers in order to initiate and also to consolidate entirely political goals.

417–28. In his *Theogony,* Hesiod mentions the names of fifty-two of the daughters of Okeanos (349–362). He also informs us that Okeanos and Doris had a total of three thousand daughters. At the beginning of hymn 2, we are told that Persephone was gathering flowers with the daughters of Okeanos in a beautiful meadow. Their names are not mentioned there. The poet reserves mention of their names until this later point in the hymn, in the emotional account of the reunion of Persephone with her mother. Most of the names he chooses to mention are suggestive of feminine beauty. Athena and Artemis, both virgin goddesses, were playing with the young maidens. That Styx, who has an ugly side to her, should be among them and should also be in the Hesiodic list is somewhat of a surprise. Perhaps the idea is that she should not be omitted from the list because she could be vengeful. It may also be that the Styx of this bevy of young women is not the same as the river of the underworld. The poet's choice to mention all this closer to the end of the poem creates a crescendo that testifies to the power of his memory and is very good strategy.

430–33 and 376–84. The image of Death coming and snatching someone away continues to be rich and alive in the folk songs of Greece. Hades, now called Charos, frequently comes on horseback. We do have quite a few cases in folk songs in which Charos violently abducts beautiful young women to take them to his abysmally dark kingdom. The formulaic expression "he grabbed the young woman by her hair" is not rare. Charos, then, acts very much like a robber. He is violent and impervious to all entreaties. In the iconography of the Orthodox Church, Archangel Michael is the angel of Death. He is winged and carries a deadly sword. He takes the lives of people and herds them sometimes to heaven and other times to the infernal depths below. The blending of pre-Christian and Christian elements here is indicative of the process of syncretism between pagan and Christian ideas. A few parts of Greece adopted the Christian faith quite late. Such concepts and images are now disappearing; hence, there is all the more reason to study them before they vanish altogether.

438–40. Soon after Persephone and her mother meet, Hekate approaches them and embraces Persephone. From this time on, Hekate becomes Persephone's attendant. She volunteers to be a watchful guardian, one especially aware of women's intimate problems. Quite obviously, Hekate can protect Persephone from her innocence. The violated *korê* (maiden) can ill afford to pick flowers in the company of other young women again. For Hekate, see Hesiod *Theogony* 411ff. The association of Hekate with Demeter and Persephone is understandable. She is frequently confused with Artemis and closely associated with Selene (Moon), whose role in women's menstrual cycles does not need elaboration.

450. Rharion has not been identified with a definite place in the vicinity of Eleusis, where Stephanus Byzantinus (1849) places it. "Udder of the earth" is a poetic way of referring to land that is very productive, nurturing men the way a mother does. "Omphalos" ("navel") and Delphoi itself both stand for the uterus of the earth. "Udder" here may indeed point to a very old mythological idea according to which

Hellas (Greece) is like a cow, perhaps a sacrificial cow, to her sons and daughters (see Athanassakis 2001a, 299–301).

460. Demeter is the daughter of Kronos and Rhea.

476. The Greek word that I translate as "celebration" is "drêsmosynê" ("enactment"); thus, the emphasis is definitely on a sacred *drama* in which the story of Demeter and Persephone was acted out by priests and priestesses of the cult.

479. The *hierokêryx* (literally, sacred herald) proclaimed silence with the word "euphê-meite" ("keep reverent silence"), and the initiates complied. The injunction not to divulge the sacred rites must rather refer to the sworn secrecy that was imposed upon the initiates. The reasons for this secrecy are not immediately obvious. Religious or semireligious societies still swear their members to secrecy on certain aspects of their initiations and their practices. Some scholars have supposed that the *drômena* (which we may translate as rituals of the Eleusinian mysteries) were kept secret because their revelation would rob them of their power. Others have seen in these mysteries an ancient chthonic cult of the original inhabitants of Eleusis, who were anxious to keep it secret from their Indo-European conquerors. I think that secrecy was imposed in order to protect the rites from vulgarization and frivolous mimicry and to keep them as the private preserve, as it were, of the few families from which the priests of this prestigious cult were drawn.

480–82. For the sentiment, see Aristophanes *Frogs* 455–59; Pindar fragment 137 (Snell and Maehler 1987); Plato *Phaedrus* 69c; and Euripides *Herakles* 613ff. The bliss of the initiates may have stemmed from their communion with divinities connected with the whole cycle of life from birth to death and from their participation in holy rites that revealed to them that death was only part of this cycle and not the end of it.

480–83. The emphasis in these lines is on seeing and witnessing the mysteries in person. The cult of Demeter at Eleusis was a mystical one. In such cults, various secret religious symbols and texts are revealed to the initiates.

483–95. Demeter and Persephone went to

Olympos to take their place in the divine assembly. This joint visit raises some questions. Persephone is not an Olympian goddess. She is the daughter of Zeus and Demeter. It is almost as if this one time she is received as an honorary guest. Demeter is Zeus's sister and the granddaughter of Gaia. Incestuous relations among the gods may involve the idea that choice was severely limited.

489. In Orphic hymn 40.3, Demeter is described as *ploutodoteira* (giver of wealth; "ploutos" means "wealth" in Greek), and in the *Thesmophoriazousai* of Aristophanes (296), Ploutos is invoked in prayer after Demeter and Persephone. In art, Ploutos is often represented as a boy with a cornucopia or a corn-basket. One may conjecture that in addition to psychic bliss and hope for an afterlife, the initiates were also promised material wealth as a reward for their participation in the sacred rites.

490–95. These lines constitute a prayer comparable to prayers found in the Orphic Hymns. The poet appeals to Demeter and Persephone to grant him wealth. See also Orphic hymn 40 to Demeter.

491. The cult of Demeter at Paros is well known both from inscriptions and other evidence. The scholiast on the *Birds* of Aristophanes informs us that Archilochos, an important lyrical poet of the seventh century BC had composed a hymn to Parian Demeter. Antron was a Thessalian town mentioned in *Iliad* 2.697.

3 : To Apollon

Jealousy prevents Hera from coming to the assistance of Leto when Leto gives birth to Apollon on the island of Delos. The goddesses who do come to Delos to help the new mother belong to the generation of the Titans. Leto herself is a Titaness. Sometimes, when Zeus is the father, the offspring is eventually granted Olympian status. The assembled goddesses send Iris to Olympos to ask the Olympian gods to dispatch Eileithyia to Delos. Eileithyia, the goddess who eases the travail of birth, returns with Iris—the two walking like trembling doves. Leto embraces a palm tree and kneels on the grassy meadow as the earth below smiles, and the newborn baby takes small

steps and runs toward the light. Leto does not nurse the baby. Themis pours nectar and ambrosia for him, and Leto rejoices for giving birth to a mighty son.

Apollon, handsomest of the Greek gods, was also a model for Greek youths when they attained early manhood. The etymology of the god's name remains unknown. His protective, especially healing power extends over many areas of life. As is evident from his powerful presence at Epidauros, he heals those who come to him properly prepared through purification. At this site, he was eventually succeeded by his son, Asklepios.

The widespread motif of a god or hero slaying a monster is central to the establishment of the cult of Apollon at Delphoi. This myth existed in the traditions of many other peoples, foremost in Ugaritic, Mesopotamian, Hittite, and Hurrian myths. In Norse mythology, Thor, the thunder god, kills the serpent that threatens the cosmic order. Legend has Apollon spend six months of the year among the Hyperboreans. It also speaks of priestesses from the extreme north who come to Delos each year, bearing precious gifts (Herodotos 4.33–35 and Pindar *Pythian Ode* 10.30). The mounted Saint George who kills the dragon has inherited aspects and functions of Apollon. The main places of his worship are Delos, Epidauros, and Delphoi. All of them are built away from big cities. Apollon is a distant god. He does not encourage humans to come near him, maybe because human beings are mortal and mortality carries with it the risk of pollution. Usually Apollon does not share cult space with Artemis, his sister. There is some principle of balance in space arrangements.

The *Hymn to Apollon* has come down to us as the second longest and the oldest of the thirty-three Homeric Hymns. We have both the name of the author and the date of composition on the authority of the Sicilian chronicler Hippostratos (third century BC). Hippostratos tells us that the author was a certain Kynaithos from the island of Chios, "who first recited the poems of Homer at Syracuse in the sixty-ninth Olympiad." Scholars find no objection to the name of the poet, but they consider the date given (504 BC) as far too late to explain certain glaring omissions in the poem. The most prominent among these are the Pytheia, the splendid Pytheian games, which became Panhellenic, the chasm, the burning of the first Delphic temple, and the building of the temple to Apollon on the island of Delos. The hymn must antedate the burning of the Delphic temple in 548 BC (for this temple, which was built by Trophonios and Agamedes, see lines 294–99). The rhapsode Kynaithos may have recited from the Homeric epics in Syracuse shortly after the foundation of that city in 733 BC. He also may have composed the *Hymn to Apollon* earlier, perhaps in the middle of the eighth century BC. If this not unreasonable conjecture is true, our poet was a contemporary of Hesiod and of Eumelos of Corinth. In keeping with rhapsodic practice, Kynaithos must have composed the hymn as a *prooimion* (prelude) to the recitation of longer portions from the Homeric epics. It is perhaps due to this fact that confusion arose as to the authorship of the preludes. They were Homeric in style and preceded the recitation of truly Homeric pieces by rhapsodes, who frequently referred to themselves as Homeridae, the sons or simply followers of Homer.

The fact that a portion of the hymn is dedicated to the Delian Apollon and another longer portion to the Delphic Apollon has led some scholars to propound the theory that we are dealing with two poems by two different authors or, at least, with two poems by the same author. The separatists consider line 178 the last line of one hymn and line 179 the beginning of another. Internal evidence from the poem has been marshaled forth to support this theory, and a misunderstood passage from Thucydides 3.104 has added to the confusion. What the separatists have failed to understand is that the poet of the hymn was not a professor of history or archaeology but a bard schooled in the digressive, leisurely, and frequently omissive manner of the epic tradition. He composed his poem in order to please and entertain pilgrims and festive celebrants rather than to satisfy the demands of literary critics and poetic surgeons. This is not to say that the poet of the hymn does not teach us much about history, archaeology,

and religion. Quite the contrary. But he also teaches us much about Apollon as the Greeks imagined him and felt his divine power. Today's approach, subject as it is to the dictates of another age, will not concede that Apollon changed into a dolphin or that he slew the dragon at Delphoi. A Greek peasant, whose gods and saints still perform such miracles, will have no trouble believing the poet. Thus, the poet of our hymn can communicate with much less trouble with the Greek peasant than with the learned specialist. The visitor—or rather the pilgrim—who goes to Delos or Delphoi will do well to lend the poet a gentle and reverent ear, because the poet tells the truth, the religious and poetic truth.

Apollon comes to the aid of those who worship him and take care of his temples, but he is also a punitive god. Some memory of Apollon Helios, the sun god, is preserved in shrines and small temples built on mountain peaks in Greece. We have a blending of the old and the not so old in such places of devotion, where the prophet Elijah, now frequently called Ai-Lias, has succeeded Apollon Helios. Much like Apollon Helios, in the iconography of the Orthodox Church the assumption of the prophet Elijah shows him riding a flaming chariot drawn by horses.

1–4. The poet introduces Apollon as the archer par excellence. When he strings his bow, the gods are startled. (For a far more elaborate passage on stringing a bow, see *Odyssey* 21.409ff.) Leto, the mother of Apollon and Artemis, is a Titaness and a daughter of Phoibe and Koios (Hesiod *Theogony* 404–10). Not many Titans are worshipped in historical times, but Leto was frequently worshipped either together with her two children or separately (e.g., on Delos and Phaistos, where there was a Lêtôon, a temple dedicated to Leto).

14–18. In these lines, the poet tips his hat, as it were, to Apollon's mother, as it is quite proper to show respect to Leto, who is not only the mother of Apollon but also a goddess herself. It is interesting that the poet of our hymn has her seated among the Olympians. This is due more to the author's imagination and his desire to elevate her position than to any traditional inclusion of Leto in the Olympian pantheon. Both Homer and Hesiod know that Leto is the mother of Apollon and Artemis (see Homer *Iliad* 1.9 and 36; 16.849; 24.605ff.; and Hesiod *Theogony* 918–20), but they do not give us an account of the circumstances of their birth. Some have identified the name Ortygiê (16) with the Syracusan Ortygia. The Greek geographer Strabo identified it with Rheneia, a small island near Delos (see *Odyssey* 15.403–4). It should be mentioned here that other places besides Delos, such as Lykia and Ephesos, claimed to have been Apollon's birthplace. Leto leaned against Kynthos, a low-lying hill (17) and thus clearly was imagined to have born the god at the foot of this granite elevation near the famous and well-attested palm tree and the mostly dry stream of the Inopos (18), which has been identified in modern times by Ross (1924). (For the river Inopos and the general topography of Delos see Stillwell, MacDonald, and McAllister [1976], s.v. "Delos.") It is interesting that on the top of Kynthos, Zeus, Apollon, and Artemis shared both a cult and the epithet Kynthios, and that the Diana Cynthia of later times was thought to have been born together with Apollon on Delos.

22. It has been conjectured, and with good reason, that the Christianized Greeks have so frequently built temples to the prophet Elijah (Elias in modern Greek) on mountain peaks and hilltops because of the partial homonymy between his name and that of Apollon Helios, now pronounced Ilios.

27–28. The wave is a portent attending the miraculous birth.

30–44. These lines read like a pilgrim's guide to Apollon's shrines. But, although most of the places mentioned did have Apollonian cults, the manner in which the places are listed draws more attention to the extent of Leto's wanderings. According to legend, the Athenian hero Theseus founded the Delian festival in honor of Apollon on his return to Athens from Crete. There were many places named Aigai in ancient Greece. The one mentioned in line 32 may be an island near Euboea (Flach 1883 s.v. "Hesychius"). The identification of Eiresiai (32) with Pliny's Irrhesia on the Thermaic gulf (*Natural History* 4.72) is very doubtful. Peparêthos

(32) is next to Skiathos in the northwest Aegean (now on the map as Skopelos). Thracian Samos (34) is surely Samothrace in the north Aegean, and Ida, of course, is not the Cretan Ida but Homer's Trojan Ida. Phôkaia (35) was on the coast of Asia Minor, southeast of Lesbos, and Autokanê may have been situated also on the coast of Asia Minor opposite the south point of Lesbos. Imbros and Lêmnos are on the northwest corner of the Aegean and easy to find on the map. Lêmnos is called by its Greek name, while Imbros, which now belongs to Turkey, appears on maps as Imroz or Gökçeada. Makar (37), usually known as Makareus, was discovered by his father, Aiolos, to have an incestuous relationship with his sister (Ovid *Heroides* 11; Hyginus *Fabula* 242). For Makar as ruler and lawgiver on Lesbos, see Diodorus Siculus 5.82. Mimas (39) was in the Erythraean peninsula and opposite Chios, and Kôrykos (39) was the south promontory of the same peninsula. Klaros (40), located near the city of Kolophôn on the coast of Asia Minor near modern Tsille, had both an oracle and a temple dedicated to Apollon. Aisageê (40) has not been identified. Mount Mykalê (41) was opposite Samos on the coast of Asia Minor. Those who are curious about the relationship of Meropes (42) to "meropes" ("mortal") in the Greek epic might wish to read H. Koller's excellent article in *Glotta*, 46, 1968, 18ff. Both Knidos and Karpathos (43) had Apollonian cults. Rhênaia (44), usually spelled Rhên(e)ia, is the much larger island west of Delos.

It may not be irrelevant at this point to mention that there are close to five hundred epithets attached to Mary, the mother of Jesus, throughout the Hellenic world. Most of them are of toponymic origin. The emphasis on mentioning so many islands may be religious in character. Naxos and Paros are listed in line 44 among the many islands that feared to play host to Leto and her splendid divine child. Leto went to Delos, before Apollon was born, and asked the island to serve as Apollon's seat of worship. Delos accepted this noble mission.

Naxos started erecting a huge temple to Apollon on the island of Palatia, at the entrance to its main harbor. Regrettably,

Christian fanatics destroyed what they could in the sixth and seventh centuries AD and built a church on the site. It is sad that Christian fanatics swept through the Delphic temple as well and finished off what was left from the destructive actions of the Roman Emperor Theodosius.

47. The places that Leto visited refused to be Apollon's birthplace because they feared the angry jealousy of Hera. Pausanias tells us that, according to Tegean legend, the reluctant offenders were later punished by Apollon and Artemis (8.53.1). In another version of the same story, Leto traveled in the form of a she-wolf from the land of the Hyperboreans to Delos in twelve days (Aristotle *Historia animalium* 580A; Aelian *Natura animalium* 4.4 and 11.1). The bronze statue of a she-wolf shown at Delphoi in ancient times was doubtless connected with this story.

58. Hecatombs, originally sacrifices of a hundred oxen, were especially connected with the worship of Apollon, and Ionian communities named a month, Hekatombaiôn, after the festival of Apollon Hekatombaios.

64–65. The poet is most likely giving us his version of the etymology of the name of the island by implying a derivation from the root "dêl"—seen in "dêleomai" ("to harm") and "dêlêeis" ("baneful"). The most probable view, and one held by some of the ancients, is that Delos means "clear, conspicuous."

73–75. The idea that Delos was a floating island up to the birth of Apollon comes later than the date of composition of this hymn, and these lines do not contain a hidden reference to what must have been a product of poetic fancy.

79–82. The oracle on Delos, attested by a single inscription (*IG* XI.2.165V.44), must have sunk into insignificance and obscurity so early that our classical sources are virtually silent on it.

84–86. For the solemnity of the oath, see *Iliad* 15.36–37. The Styx is invoked as a dread representative of underworld powers, which sanction the oath and may also visit the perjurer with punishment.

92–96. Most of the goddesses named in these lines have a place among the Titans (see Hesiod *Theogony* 135 and Apollodoros 1.1.3).

The phrase "other immortal goddesses" of line 95 is rather vague, and we cannot but notice the chthonic character of the attending divinities. Ichnaian Themis (94) had few cults, but she was present at the birth of Athena (Paus. 3.17.3) and of Aphrodite (Paus. 5.11.8).

97. Eileithyia is the divine midwife and daughter of Zeus and Hera (Hesiod *Theogony* 922). In Homer, she is controlled by Hera, who delays the birth of Herakles by preventing Eileithyia from attending (*Iliad* 19.119). In historical times, Eileithyia was worshipped not only on Delos but also throughout the Cyclades, Crete, and the mainland.

102. Iris is regularly used as divine messenger (see *Hymn to Demeter* 2.314).

117. The palm tree of the holy precinct of Apollon is mentioned in *Odyssey* 6.162 and was reported as still alive in the days of Cicero (*Laws* 1.1) and of Pliny (*Natural History* 16.89). The image is intended to show Leto's supernatural height and strength.

117–18. Statues of kneeling women about to give birth and of goddesses of birth suggest that this position was commonly assumed by laboring women in ancient Greece.

124. In the *Hymn to Demeter* (2.237), Demeter anoints Demophoön with ambrosia in order to make him immortal. Aristaios is made immortal by feeding on nectar and ambrosia (Pindar *Pythian Ode* 9.63).

127–29. For the precocity of the divine infant, see *Hymn to Hermes* 4.15–19.

136–38. These lines are found in only some of the manuscripts.

146–57. By the end of the fifth century BC, the Ionians no longer flocked to Delos for this great festival but instead gathered at Ephesos on the Asiatic coast. Thucydides reports that adversities, which he does not specify, were responsible for the waning of this splendid festival (see Thuc. 3.104). We may conjecture that as the Delphic festival grew in importance, the Delian festival must have slowly declined in inverse proportion. The Delian chorus took part in other festivals and also performed on the occasion of sacred embassies to the sanctuary.

157–64. The Delian maidens obviously followed a certain hierarchic order in their performance. They started with a hymn

to Apollon, Artemis, and Leto, the divine
mother; then they sang a song in praise
of heroes. Finally, in what must have been
mimetic sketches in the various dialects
of the pilgrims, they provided them with
light-hearted entertainment. The sequence
was thus in descending order (gods-
heroes-men), and in typical Greek fashion
the solemnity of the festival was tempered
with a note of frivolity at the end.

165–78. In these lines, the poet asks the Delian
maidens to make him the poet laureate, as
it were, of the Delian festival. In exchange
he promises to make their skill in song
known far and wide and never to "cease
to hymn Far-shooting Apollon." Given the
conventions of early Greek epic poetry, the
directness of the poet is remarkable. There
is no doubt that contests were held during
the Delian festival. The Hesiodic fragment
265 teaches us this much:

> First then Homer and I as singers com-
>   posed song
> in youthful hymns in which we sang
> of Phoibos Apollon of the golden sword,
> Apollon to whom Leto gave birth.

Lines 171–73 must have originated the
tradition that Homer was a blind poet
from Chios. Combining lines 165–78 with
the above fragment 265, one might for a
moment imagine that, if the blind poet of
our hymn was Homer, Hesiod might well
be his competitor, but unfortunately this
enticing conjecture would meet with a wall
of formidable objections.

179–80. These are Apollon's Asiatic haunts and
as such most welcome to those who hold
the view that Apollon came to Greece from
Asia. Some scholars have connected Lykia
(Lycia) with the cult epithet lyk(e)ios and
Lykêgenês (*Iliad* 4.101). But opinions are divided. Some scholars think that these words
basically stem from the toponym "Lykiê."
Others, depending on their views about the
origin of Apollon, connect their root with
that of the Latin "lux" ("light"). This is a
sufficiently attractive derivation, but it does
not satisfy those who see the Greek word
"lykos" ("wolf" or "an animal with gleaming
eyes") as more probable linguistic kin of the
disputed epithets. Patara, where the god was
thought to spend six months of the year,

was in Lydia, while Karia (Caria) boasted
of a famous Apollonian oracle at Didyma to
the south of Miletos. Farther north were the
famous oracle and temple at Klaros (Ionia)
and a similar combination of shrine and
oracle at Gryneion (Aeolia).

188–89. See pseudo-Hesiodic *Shield* 201–06
and Pindar *Nemean Ode* 5.22. In the *Shield*,
we have a reference to the sacred ring dance.
In these lines the Muses are leading the
song and Apollon plays his lyre beautifully.
In the Pindaric passage of *Nemean Ode*,
Apollon plays the lyre and the Muses sing
popular wedding songs.

194. The Graces (Charites) and the Seasons
(Horae) are most frequently associated with
Aphrodite (see *Iliad* 5.338; *Odyssey* 18.194;
Cypria 5). The haunts of the Graces are near
those of the Muses on Olympos (Hesiod
Theogony 64), and they are associated with
Apollon in literature (Pindar *Olympian
Ode* 14.10) and in art (Paus. 9.35.1). Plutarch
(*Moralia* 1136A) tells us that on Delos there
was a statue of Apollon with the bow in his
right hand and the three Graces to his left.
The cult epithet hôromedôn (*IG* XII.5.893),
roughly translated "ruler of the Seasons," as
well as similar epithets, also shows a close
connection of Apollon with the Seasons.
The Hesiodic Horae (*Theogony* 900–903)
are daughters of Zeus and Themis, and their
names (Eunomia, Dikê, and Eirenê) point
more to their legal and pacific character.
However, in general, they were kindly
divinities associated with the changes of
the seasons and the growth of vegetation.
Their first representation is on the François
vase, and their concept has been beautifully
treated in neoclassical art (Thorvaldsen)
and music (Vivaldi).

195. Harmonia was the daughter of Ares and
Aphrodite. She was offered to Kadmos as
his wife and gave birth to the ill-fated Agave.
Her necklace played an important role in
the Theban saga. Hebe was the daughter
of Zeus and Hera. She served as cupbearer
to the gods (*Iliad* 4.2) and was given to
Herakles as his wife (*Odyssey* 11.603). She
was quite unimportant in cult.

208–13. The daughter of Azas may be Koronis
(she is usually the daughter of the Lapith
Phlegyas). We do know that Ischys, son of
Elatos, was a rival of Apollon (Hesiod fr.

125; Pindar *Pythian Ode* 3.55). Phorbas and Ereutheus may have been Apollon's rivals for the love of Koronis, but the text is such that the presence of each rival may imply a fresh object of contention. Leukippos (212) courted Daphne and approached her in the guise of a woman. This, however, did not deceive Daphne and her companions, who killed him when they discovered his gender (Paus. 8.20.3).

216. Apollon had been received on Olympos (186) before he started his search for the site of his oracle. Pieria is north of Olympos.

217. Lektos may have been a harbor or a coastal town. The Ainianes lived at the springs of the Spercheios.

218–21. The Perrhaiboi lived around Larissa in Thessaly. From Iolkos near the Pagasitic gulf, Apollon came to cape Kênaion at the extreme northwest tip of Euboea. His next stop, the Lelantine plain, is to be found between Chalkis and Eretria.

223–24. The mountain must be Messapios across from Chalkis. Mykalessos is beyond Aulis and southeast of it at the foot of Mount Messapios. Teumessos is the modern Mesovouni, a small village about five miles from Thebes.

225–28. The abode of Thebe is of course the city of Thebes. She was daughter of the river god Asopos and twin sister of Aigina. She became the bride of Zethos and gave her name to the city that was previously known as Kadmeia. Apollon's cult in Thebes must have flourished at times.

230–38. Both the grove and the temple were famous in antiquity (*Iliad* 2.506; Hesiod *Catalogue of Women* 219; Alcaeus frag. Z102 LP [7 Loeb]; Pindar *Isthmian* 1.33). Pausanias reports that when he visited the place, the town and the temple were in ruins, but the statue of Poseidon was still standing (9.26.3). The exact character and significance of the custom described in these lines are not clear. Of the many explanations offered so far, those that consider the custom a specific rite performed on a certain occasion must be closer to the truth. The rider of the chariot leaps off and allows the horse or horses to race through the trees. If the chariot is not dashed against the trees, the god does not claim it as his. But if the chariot is broken, the rider

interprets this as an indication of Poseidon's will to keep it.

240–43. The Kephissos (not to be confused with the better-known Attic stream) flowed across the northern part of lake Kopais. Okalea was near lake Kopais, and Haliartos lay between Onchestos and Okalea. In view of the location of these places, the god's itinerary is not very logical. The travels of Leto (30–45) are beset with similar problems, which stem at times from metrical necessity and at other times from a poet's approach, which cannot be the same as that of a geographer.

244. This may be the same as the Telphousa of Pausanias 9.33.1.

244ff. According to our poet, no temple was built at Telphousa. Thus, it may be futile to seek the remnants of such a temple at whichever place we identify as Telphousa.

250. "Peloponnesos," as a single word, is found here for the first time. It otherwise occurs as "Pelopos nêsos" ("island of Pelops").

251. By "Europe" here the poet seems to mean northern Greece. Since Hesiod applies the name to a nymph (*Theogony* 357), this is surely the oldest application of the name to a geographical area. Europe is not mentioned either in the *Iliad* or in the *Odyssey*. In times that preceded Homer's epics, Europe and Hellas may have been roughly coextensive, referring to the Greek northwest and specifically to the land between the upper Achelôos river and the coastline. Northern Europe, in this case all the lands roughly to the north of present-day Greece, was unknown to Herodotos (3.115–16). "Europe" is a Greek word, which means "she of the broad face" or "the broad-browed one." Homeric "eurymetôpos" ("broad-browed"), an epithet applied only to cows, is a very close analogue. A geographically displaced Europe, daughter of the king of Phoenicia, mates with a bull that is none other than Zeus. Even the story of Europe's brother Kadmos and the cow that leads him to the foundation of Thebes may be a precious remnant of a prehistoric myth in which Europe was a cow, out of whose sacrificed body the land was created. In Norse mythology, the land is created out of the hacked body of the giant Ymir, who drinks enormous amounts of milk from the teats of

the cow Audhumla (*Snorra Edda*, Gylfaging-
ing VI–VIII).

272. Iêpaiêôn here is a cult epithet for Apollon.
In lines 500 and 517 it is the name of a song
composed in honor of the god. The popular
ancient etymology of the word from "iê
Paian" may not be incorrect simply because
it was not advanced by modern linguistics.

278–80. The Phlegyes were a tribe hostile
to the Delphic precinct. Lake Kephisis is
otherwise known as Kopais (Paus. 9.24.1;
9.36.2; 10.7.1).

281–99. On Delphoi and the temple, the reader
may wish to consult Pausanias 10.5.5ff.;
Strabo 9.3; Courby *Fouilles de Delphes* 2.92.
This is not the place for a history of the
fortunes of the holy precinct, but it should
be mentioned that the original temple
was destroyed by fire or arson in 548 BC,
and that some years later, by 505 BC, the
Alcmeonids, aided by generous contribu-
tions by Amasis, Croesus, and other wealthy
barbarians and Greeks, erected at Delphoi
a splendid temple of Parian marble. For
the legendary builders Trophonios and
Agamedes (296), see Pausanias 9.37.4 and
pseudo-Platonic *Axiochos* 367c. Kris(s)a, a
few kilometers down from the Delphic hill,
attempted to control Delphoi, but it was
destroyed at the end of the First Sacred War
(585 BC).

300. We cannot be absolutely sure about the
identification of this spring, but the Castal-
ian spring seems a reasonable conjecture.

306. For Typhaôn (Typhoeus in 367), see
Hesiod *Theogony* 306ff., 820ff.

333–36. For invoking chthonic deities or ghosts
by striking the earth with the flat of the
hand, see *Iliad* 9.568; Euripides *Troiades*
1306. For the origin and ancient etymology
of the Titans (Titênes), Hesiod may be con-
sulted with profit (*Theogony* 207–10). The
battle of the gods against the Titans, the
Titanomachy, is described in majestic poetry (Hesiod *Theogony* 617ff.). The common
ancestry of gods and men occurs in Hesiod
Works and Days 108.

340–43. The earth was invoked along with the
sky in line 334 in a manner reminiscent of
similar invocations in modern Greek folk
songs. Thus, in the Cypriot wedding song,
when the wheat used for the *resin* (the
wedding meal of cracked wheat) is taken

from the spring to the home of the bride or
the bridegroom, the young man, soon to be
a husband, swears by the earth, the sky, the
stars, and the moon (see Athanassakis 1976,
especially 97–99). In lines 340–43 Hera
strikes the earth, and the earth moves in order to show that Hera's wish will be granted.
The earth is not an anthropomorphic goddess but a palpable elemental power that is
capable of hearing and responding.

352. Typhaôn and Typhoeus seem to be a
generic name for monstrous creatures. The
dread Typhaôn of Hesiod *Theogony* 820ff.
was a child of Earth (Gaia) and Tartaros.

367. Chimaira was the daughter of Typhaôn
and Echidna (Hesiod *Theogony* 306, 319).

370–74. Of all the folk etymologies that the
ancients gave in explanation of the origin of
Pythô and Pytheios, this is the oldest and
the best (see Paus. 10.6.5).

391–403. The story of the first Delphic priests'
coming from Knossos and of Apollon's
metamorphosis into a dolphin (Gr. *delphis*)
certainly shows that our poet thought that
the cult of Apollon Delphinios had strong
ties with Crete. There was a temple of Apollon Delphinios at Knossos (*CIG* II.2554,
f98), and the title *delphinios* was applied to
Apollon in votive Cretan inscriptions on
the island of Delos (*BCH* 3.293; 4.355). The
poet of the hymn must have thought that
the toponym "Delphoi" stemmed from the
fact that Apollon appeared to his priests in
the shape of a dolphin.

396. This line has made some scholars think
that the Delphic oracle was a tree oracle in
the beginning. The reader may recall that
the Selloi, priests of Dodona, practiced
divination by interpreting the rustling of
the leaves of the sacred oak. This is an
attractive conjecture, but more evidence is
needed to support it. We know that the
first Delphic temple was built of laurel, that
the priestess chewed leaves of laurel before
she uttered her prophetic words, and that
she also inhaled the smoke of burned laurel
before she descended into the cavern.

409–13. Maleia and Tainaron both were cities
situated on the homonymous promontories
of the southern Peloponnese.

422–24. For Arênê, birthplace of the Argo-
nauts Lynkeus and Idas, see *Iliad* 2.591 and
11.723; also Apollonios Rhodios 1.152. Line

423 is identical with *Iliad* 2.592. Thryon and Aipy are discussed by Strabo 8.3.24ff. Pylos of line 424 is the Triphylian one also discussed by Strabo (8.3.7ff.). Argyphea has not been identified.

425–26. Both Krounoi and Chalkis were small streams (see Strabo 8.3.13, 26ff.) in the district of Makistia to the south of the mouth of the Alpheios. Dymê, to the west of the mouth of the Peiros river and not very far from Patrai, is out of place in this catalogue. Homer also calls the inhabitants of Elis *Epeioi* (see *Iliad* 2.619; 4.537, etc.).

427–29. The identity of Pherai is doubtful. Perhaps this is an alternate spelling for Pharai in Achaia, a town by the river Peiros, halfway between Dymê and Leontion. Doulichion must be modern Leukas, and Samê modern Kephallenia. Ithakê and Zakynthos can be found almost in every map of Greece.

440–42. Apollon springs from the ship in the likeness of a star at midday, as flashes of light—literally, sparks—fly about and their intense brilliance touches the sky. Light frequently accompanies divine presence or divine energy. The light of these lines is very different from the brilliance that signals the two epiphanies of Demeter (2.188–89 and 275–80) as well as the two epiphanies of Aphrodite (5.86–90 and 172–75). In these passages, the light is gentler, more feminine. The extraordinary brilliance that emanates from Apollon as he leaps from the ship is very similar to the brilliance that envelops Athena when she leaps from the peaks of Olympos on an earthbound mission that requires speed as well as swift and resolute action (*Iliad* 4.73–78). Those interested in the semiotics of light in Homer and in the Homeric Hymns might wish to study the lines just cited in detail. *Iliad* 5.4–8; 6.295; 10.47; 11.61–66; 12.462–65; 13.240–45; 18.202–14; 19.362–67; 19.373–74; 22.315–21 offer exciting examples of both the poetics and the semiotics of light in the earliest Greek epic. Energy-filled, coruscating, aggressive light has masculine associations. One might object that the case of Athena emitting powerful stellar light argues against this thought. Such an objection cannot be sustained because, born from the head of

Zeus, this warrior-goddess has many masculine functions and attributes.

443. These would be votive tripods arranged in rows in front of the temple.

463. Ancient sources name the leader of the Cretans as Kastalios or Ikadios.

493–95. The composer of the hymn attributes the cult of Apollon Delphinios to the god's epiphany as a dolphin and seems to be of the opinion that the cult originated in Crete. Although the name Delphoi is not mentioned in the hymn, some modern scholars see the story as a mythological *aition* for the name Delphoi and thus also make an etymological connection between "delphis" ("dolphin") and Delphoi. The Greek name for the god's site of worship, Delphoi, seems to be an old locative for Delphos. Is it not possible that this word might be related to "delphys" ("womb")? Indeed, if Delphoi was the *omphalos* (navel) of the earth, it is not too daring to suggest that in some sense it and its outlying area constituted the womb, and, in a loose sense, the belly of the earth.

500. Perhaps the Iêpaiêôn was a hymn to Apollon the healer (see the root "iê" in "iê-tros," which means "physician"). For the paean, which before the First Sacred War (c. 590 BC) was the main event in a musical competition of kithara-players, see Strabo 9.3.12.

518. In *Iliad* 1.472–74 we come upon the young Achean warriors as they drink and sing a paean to Apollon all day long.

535–37. The Greeks of historical times—much as they do today about certain monasteries—were in the habit of making unkind remarks about the greed with which the Delphic priests wielded the butcher's knife. The meat, which after all could not all be consumed by the priests, was usually distributed among the inhabitants of Delphoi. Even now in Greece people offer sheep and goats to monasteries, usually to fulfill a vow. The animals are frequently slaughtered to feed everyone at major feasts. Saint George is a very popular saint. On his feast day, April 23, people still gather at churches devoted to him. On that day the shepherds of Asi Gonia, district of Chania, Crete, bring their flocks to the church of Agios Georgios Galatas to be blessed. The epithet Galatas means "bringer of milk." The animals are blessed and milked one by one, and the milk is distributed among the people.

539ff. It is impossible to tell whether line 539 has fallen victim to the ravages of time or a line following it has been altogether lost.

540–44. This is a *vaticinium ex eventu* (a prophecy after the event). There was no Cretan priesthood at Delphoi in historical times. The original priests, like many who followed them in control of the holy precinct, may have been unseated either by the local rivals, who wanted a share of the pie, or by overtaxed pilgrims, who decided that enough was enough.

546. Most of the Homeric Hymns end with this transitional formula.

4 : To Hermes

The *Hymn to Hermes* is somewhat of an oddity among the other hymns. It does not possess any of the depth and the piety that permeate many of the other hymns, especially the major hymns to Apollon and Demeter. The only other hymn that bears some remote resemblance to it is the *Hymn to Aphrodite,* in which there is a humorous strain, even though milder and rather subdued by comparison. In fact, if it were not for the characteristically Hellenic attitude of mingling humor with piety and the absurd with the profoundly serious, one might be led to consider the *Hymn to Hermes* a spoof or some sort of an early example of mock-epyllion.

In this hymn, Hermes is the trickster and thief par excellence. He is the Loki of the Greek pantheon or Coyote of the Native American traditions in North America. That this view was both old and commonly held among the Greeks rather than an innovation by the composer of the hymn is proven by the fact that Homer considered the god a thief and a patron of thieves. In *Iliad* 24.24, the gods wanted him to go and steal the body of Hector from the plain of Troy where Achilles had been abusing it. In the *Odyssey*, Autolykos, who "surpassed all other men in thievery and perjury," received his dubious talents from Hermes to whom he faithfully sacrificed as his patron (19.395–98). In Hesiod's *Works and Days,* we are told that it was Hermes who endowed Pandora with a knack for thieving, lying,

and wheedling (67–68, 77–79). But Hermes was much more than a trickster and a thief. He was a divine herald, and a *psychopompos* (a god who accompanied the souls of the dead to the underworld). Hermes was a protector of herds, and an inventor of the firedrill and of the lyre. He ruled over good luck, profit, victory at a wrestling ring, divination by lot, and protection of houses as Hermes Pylaios. In our hymn, there is no indication of his power over the dead, the wrestling ring, or the gates of houses. But all his other powers and qualities are either elaborated or at least touched upon.

The poem is a major hymnal composition intended to be comprehensive. That is why the question of unity has plagued its critics. To put it quite simply, how could the rhapsode have given the poem the unity demanded by modern critics, since he had to compose a poem not about one episode in the life of a god but rather about several episodes in the life of an erratic and elusive god whose very nature contained inherent contradictions? In fact, the poem has an amazing unity. It deals with the accomplishments of a precocious divine baby, who, in a couple of days, invents the lyre and firedrill, steals the cattle of a god, becomes skilled in divination, proves Apollon's match in arguing, and wins recognition by Zeus and a place in Olympos for himself and his mother. There is unity of time and unity of theme, the theme being inventiveness and skill in thievery and deception.

The main subject of the hymn, the theft of the divine cattle, may indeed be of old Indo-European stock (in the Vedic parallel, Ahi steals the cattle of Indra). Greek literature—one does not know whether by dependence on the hymn or by drawing on common mythological stock—was quite partial to the theft of the divine cattle. Among others, Alkaios treats it in a hymn to Hermes. Sophocles deals with it in the *Ichneutai.* Apollodoros gives his version of it in 3.10.2, and if we are to judge from Antoninus Liberalis 23, Hesiod, Apollonios Rhodios, and several others tried their hands at it.

The author and the place of composition of the hymn remain unknown. Not much emphasis can be placed on the invention of the seven-stringed lyre as an aid for dating the hymn. This type of lyre was known in Crete in the Bronze Age, and its introduction to Greece must have been very early. The Triphylian Pylos, which is mentioned in this hymn (342, 355, 398) as the place to which Hermes drove the cattle, was destroyed in the so-called Second Messenian War in the last quarter of the seventh century. Of course, nothing could have prevented a poet of the fifth century from working with an earlier tradition, but chances are that the composition of the hymn antedates the destruction of Triphylian Pylos and should therefore be placed tentatively somewhere in the middle of the seventh century.

Hermes was a god of shepherds whose very primitive origins go back to the cairn (the stone heap) and its indwelling *numen*. Cairns can still be found in the remote mountains of Epirus, Crete, and even Boeotia. Their ancient functions have been forgotten. In very old times the stone heap may have served both as a burial mound as well as a border mark. The spirit that lived in the stone heap protected the place upon which it was erected and the rights of those who erected it. Perhaps a single sharp and protruding stone was emblematic of the sexual prowess of the clan or tribe that claimed the stone heap, threatening violators with sexual outrage. The spirit was given human form and eventually became the elegant divine messenger we encounter in *Odyssey* 5.43–54. The god's name and practically all the obscure epithets that describe his attributes point to pastoral origins. Hermes, past his most primitive stage, is nothing more than the prototypical shepherd euhemerized. He is a pathbreaker and a pathfinder. He can steal cattle, and hence, he can protect shepherds against cattle theft. Like most shepherds, he is swift-footed. In fact, aided by his winged cap and winged sandals, he can fly. The staff he carries is a shepherd's staff put to the service of new, higher functions.

The new, more evolved shepherd-god would of course be the one to herd flocks of souls to their proper resting place and to stand at the entrance of sheep pens and dwellings, in carved effigy, aiming his erect phallus at unwelcome visitors, especially thieves. Before he was elevated to Olympian status, Hermes must have helped shepherd clans and individuals to communicate with one another by appearing in dreams and visions, and by gifting fleet-footed shepherds with the inspiration and the power to run long distances to deliver important messages.

The presence of Hermes in the gymnasia promoted the idea of defiance and masculinity. These aspects and functions of the god are left out of the Homeric hymn. Hermes is the only god who ventures into the dark kingdom of Hades. His ability to cross boundaries and his magical staff with which he puts men to sleep and also wakes them up suggest a possible connection with Shamanism. The Roman coordinate of Hermes was Mercurius, a god introduced to the Roman world most likely from ancient Gall. Words such as "mark" ("merk") bear witness to his original function. Further, it is possible that Hermes is etymologically related to the Germanic word "Irminsul" ("Irmin's Pillar"). Many obscure epithets are attached to the various functions of the god. However, upon closer inspection they turn out not to be so very obscure. As *eriounios* the god may help sheep and goats have longer hair. *Diaktoros* may refer to the god's assistance to shepherds in breaking a path through thick scrub and forest. For more details, see Athanassakis (1989b).

In the present hymn, Hermes performs extraordinary deeds when he is still but a little baby. Readers will recall how the infant Herakles strangled snakes that were sent by a jealous Hera to strangle him. Of course, there is unusual exaggeration in all this. A cattle thief must first build a reputation for his skills and his daring. So Hermes must perform some extraordinary deeds before he is taken seriously. He must also learn how to settle with those who have power. See Herzfeld (1985).

Hermes was almost everywhere. As a god of shepherds, he protected them and their flocks against cattle thieves, but he was also a god to whom cattle thieves could pray for success. On the one hand, he was the elegant messenger described in *Odyssey* 5.43–50, but also the naked athlete sculpted by famous sculptors. As such, he attracted the wrath of early fanatic Christians.

1. Maia, the daughter of Atlas, is important only as the mother of Hermes. Her name means "mother" or "nurse," and in the *Odyssey* she is one of the Pleiades (14.435; see also Hesiod *Theogony* 938).

2. Although several other places claimed to be the birthplace of the god, by and large tradition and literature granted the honor to Mount Kyllene in Arcadia.

15. Once more, the reference here is to the Hermai, busts of Hermes on square bases from which an erect phallus projected. They stood at the entrances of private houses and temples in Athens as apotropaic guardians, and the importance attached to them by the Athenians can be gathered from the consternation that followed their mutilation on the eve of the Sicilian expedition in 415 BC.

19. The division of the month here is bipartite, and this is the first fourth day of the first half of the month. Hesiod reckons simply by days, by a tripartite division into decades, and by a bipartite division into waxing and waning moons. He does not associate the fourth of the month with the birth of Hermes, but he considers it a lucky day (for details, see *Works and Days* 765ff.). In classical times, the fourth was a lucky day, and both Hermes and Aphrodite were thought to have been born on it.

24. In other sources (Apollodoros 3.10.2; Sophocles *Ichneutai*; and Eratosthenes *Katasterismoi* 24), the episode of the tortoise follows the theft and slaughter of the cows. This change in the sequence of events must be due to a desire to make it logical: if Hermes slaughtered the cows first, he would have a supply of strings for his lyre.

30–38. The words of Hermes are, of course, ironic, and the passage has a good bit of comic levity with which the entire hymn is permeated. Line 36 is a proverb that occurs in Hesiod *Works and Days* 365. A pun is doubtless intended, since the tortoise, much like the snail, carries its home. For the tortoise as a charm (37), see Pliny *Natural History* 32.14. Turtles make little squeaky sounds when they copulate, but are otherwise silent. The idea that the animal was voiceless when alive and "vocal" when dead was comically exploited (see *Ichneutai* 292ff.).

47–54. This is the oldest passage on the construction of the lyre. See extensive articles on ancient music in *The Oxford Classical Dictionary* (Hornblower, Spawforth, and Eidinow 2012), *The History of Musical Instruments* (Sachs 1940, 129–35), and Aign (1963, passim through the index). Of the ancient passages, *Ichneutai* 302ff., Bion 5.8, and Nicander *Alexipharmaka* 560ff. are the most interesting.

54–56. Poetical improvisations of this kind are still performed at folk festivals in Greece.

57–67. The transition from singing of the union of Zeus and Maia to conceiving a plan for robbing Apollon of his cattle is abrupt, and perhaps the poet intended to show us that the god's native propensities obsessed him to the point that orderly rational thought yielded to mischievous impulse.

70. Even though there is justified suspicion for thinking that Pieria here has supplanted an earlier Pêreitê, for the time being we are forced to be content with identifying this place with the well-known Pieria north of Olympos.

71. The reader will remember that in lines 18 and 22 the cattle belong to Apollon. Here we are told that they are the property of the gods. In Homer, Apollon does not own cows or oxen. The cattle that were eaten by the men of Odysseus (*Odyssey* 1.8; 12.127ff.) belonged to Helios. Perhaps originally the cattle belonged to Helios, the Sun, and then to Apollon-Helios, the sun god.

77. Horse thieves of my native Epirus employed this ruse to evade their pursuers as late as the early twentieth century (see Vergil *Aeneid* 8.210; Livy 1.7; *Ichneutai* 110ff.).

88. Onchestos is to the northwest of Thebes.

90. The scene is reminiscent of *Odyssey* 24.227, where Laertes is digging around his vines.

99–100. If the Titan Pallas is meant, he was the son of Krios and Eurybiê (Hesiod *Theogony* 375–76). His brother Persês was the father of Hekate (*Theogony* 377, 409). This might make the Hesiodic Pallas a rather likely candidate for the father of Selene, but Hesiod clearly tells us that Helios and Selene were the children of Hyperion and Theia (371–74). Megamedes is otherwise unknown.

102. This is the well-known Alpheios river that flows into the sea near Epitalion, west of

Olympia, and on the western shore of the Peloponnese.

108–15. This is the first occurrence in Greek literature of making fire by means of a drill. (For other accounts, see Theophrastos in *Peri Phytôn Historea* 5.9.6; the scholiast on Apollonios Rhodios 1.1184; and Pliny *Natural History* 16.8).

124–26. Apollon found the hides when he was searching for his cattle (403–4). The hides that were exhibited to pilgrims could be either natural rocks vaguely suggesting the shape of an oxhide or stones hewn to that shape by human hand.

128–29. The obvious inference is that the portions correspond to the twelve Olympians, but there are some difficulties in assuming that the number of the Olympians was fixed when this hymn was composed.

127–37. Some scholars have thought that Hermes does not eat the meat that he roasted to conform with the chthonic side of his character. We know that victims were offered to him at Kyllene and that animal sacrifices to him are attested by Homer (*Odyssey* 14.435; 19.396–98). Hermes is a god and, of course, he does not eat meat. He drinks nectar and eats ambrosia. The statement that it was a craving for meat that made him steal the cattle is humorous. In the *Odyssey*, Kalypso serves Odysseus a meal such as mortals eat. She herself, sits across from him and eats ambrosia and drinks nectar (5.192–202).

148. When Pausanias visited the site, the temple of Hermes on top of Kyllene was in ruins (8.17.1). The cave mentioned here has not been identified.

186–87. This is the grove near the temple of Poseidon, for which see notes on *Hymn to Apollon* 3.230–38.

188. "Bulwark of his vineyard" is a parody of the Homeric "bulwark of the Achaeans" (said of Ajax in *Iliad* 1.282) and "bulwark of Olympos" (said of Ares in 8.3).

216. This is the Triphylian Pylos.

226. The reference is to Hermes's steps. He obviously skidded from one side of the road to the other.

231. The scent emanates from the divine presence. The Greeks still attribute the quality of divine fragrance to many of their saints.

294–98. Sneezing was considered an omen by the ancient Greeks, but the breaking of

wind must have been as much a taboo then as it is today. Hermes's behavior is virtually infantile, but the trick proved to be a temporarily effective stratagem. In the *Apocolocyntosis Divi Claudii*, Seneca may indeed have had these lines in mind when he chose Hermes as the divine agent who relieved Claudius of his flatulent travail (*Apocol.* 3).

324. For the "scales of justice" in Homer, see *Iliad* 8.69; 16.658; 19.223; 22.209.

409. A lacuna is suspected after this line. Some scholars have supposed that Apollon wanted to bind Hermes. In no way can the text yield this meaning. Apollon intended to tie his cattle and bring them back to Pieria. For using withes to tie animals, see *Odyssey* 9.427.

415. Another lacuna seems probable here.

426–33. See Hesiod *Theogony* 1–21. For Mnemosyne and her nine daughters, the Muses, see *Theogony* 52–63. Line 430 means that Mnemosyne obtained Hermes by lot, because his musical skill definitely fell within her province.

450–52. Although in 3.131 Apollon says "may the lyre (*kithara*) be dear to me," he is not claiming to have invented the instrument. According to Pausanias 9.30.1, Hermes and Apollon contested for the lyre. Nonetheless, the credit for the invention of the lyre incontrovertibly belongs to Hermes.

460. Neither in art nor in literature is Apollon usually depicted as carrying a spear. Here he is justified because he is after the robbers who stole his cattle (see *Odyssey* 14.531). In *Iliad* 1.234, Achilles swears by his scepter, that is, by the symbol of his kingly authority. Apollon's oath by the cornel spear, which can hardly be taken as a symbol of his divine power, is in keeping with the comic character of much of this hymn.

480–89. The artistic sensitivity and the truly genteel nature of the advice that Hermes gives Apollon are remarkable. It is small wonder that the best practitioners of the art of singing and playing the lyre were called *theioi* (divine). Demodokos in *Odyssey* 8.43 and 47 is a good example.

508. In many parts of Greece, the cults of the two gods were closely connected, and this line is a mere confirmation of a well-known fact.

511–12. Hermes invented the pipe and Pan, his

son, became so famous for playing it that
many students of the classics commit the
venial error of crediting Pan with the invention (see Apollodoros 3.10.2).

526. A line is missing after 526.

529–32. Surely the *kêrykeion* (herald's staff) is
meant here. With it, we are told in both the
Iliad and the *Odyssey,* the god puts men to
sleep and wakes them up (see *Iliad* 24.343–
44; *Odyssey* 24.1–5). On the other hand, in
these lines Apollon gives Hermes the staff
as a token of powers far more extensive than
we ascribe to Hermes of classical times.

541–49. Men are to inquire at the oracle only if
the omens are auspicious and then only to
a point that the god considers proper. This
relationship, as well as Apollon's bringing
good to some men and harm to others, rests
on a justification that is moral only in the
etymological sense of the word. Apollon, in
fact, declares, "I am the divine lawgiver and
things are right only so far as they conform
to the law as I lay it down; to ask more than
that of me is illegal." The Muses tell the
truth only when they want (Hesiod *Theogony* 27ff.), and Euripides also tells us that it is
ignorance to try to force the gods to reveal
what they do not wish to (*Ion* 374ff.).

552–63. The three awesome sisters who
fly about like bees and whose heads are
besprinkled with white barley flour (see
the practice of the basket-carrying maidens
in Arist. *Ekklesiazousai* 732) must be the
Thriai, eponymous nymphs of the *thriai*
(pebbles used for divination); see Apollodoros 3.10.2 and Cicero *De Divinatione*
1.34. We have no depiction of the Thriai in
art, and we do not know either how pebbles
were used in divination or how the apiform
Thriai became mantic after eating honey.

These three mysterious sisters are obviously apiform. The bee was an emblem of
Potnia, the Minoan-Mycenean goddess. The
three bee-like sisters of the present hymn
gather fresh and wild honey. It seems reasonable to assume that an additive of flower and
yeast could produce mead (*methu*). In Norse
mythology the Mead of Poetry was prepared
from the blood of the wise being Kvasir and
turned the drinker into a poet and a scholar.

568. There is a lacuna after this line.

569–71. The concept of Hermes as lord of
wild beasts is rather extravagant and almost

hyperbolic. He had power over domesticated
herds and especially sheep, and sacrifices were offered to him so that he might
increase the flocks (see *Odyssey* 14.435;
Hesiod *Theogony* 444–47).

572. Hermes was not only escort of souls on
their journey to the underworld but also
messenger of the gods.

5 : To Aphrodite

Aphrodite shares her luminous character
with many Indic divinities of fertility and
certainly with the Norse Gerd, the deified
consort of Frey. As a feminine divinity of
fertility and love, Frey has closer analogues
in Norse mythology (Freya, Frigg, Gerd).
In the Paris–Helen and Zeus–Hera (Dios
Apatê) amorous episodes (*Iliad* 3 and 14, re-
spectively), Aphrodite's principal functions
are to instill desire in male and female lovers
and, directly or indirectly, to hide them. The
mist or haze in the Paris–Helen episode and
the golden cloud in which Zeus envelops
himself and Hera are not compelling evidence for any special association of the goddess of love with clouds. Also, Aphrodite's
radiance and the golden chariot by which
she is carried through the air (Sappho, frag.
1 LP) are not unique to Aphrodite in the
Greek tradition, or to Uśas (dawn goddess)
in Indic mythology. Although one can
produce instances in which most likely syncretism links such features with chthonic
deities, they are, as one sees especially in the
Indic tradition, attributes of celestial gods.
Aphrodite's chariot in Sappho's fragment 1
is drawn by sparrows, birds that were noto-
rious for fecundity and wantonness. It will
also be remembered that, as we know from
abundant evidence in literature and art, it is
the dove that is emblematic of Aphrodite.
Both birds are doubtless symbols of erotic
desire and fertility, but whereas the dove
may have been borrowed from the cult of
Astarte, the sparrow-drawn chariot is most
likely Indo-European.

Our Homeric Aphrodite is a goddess
of love and fertility. She has no connection with earth and vegetation. We should
not forget that the Indo-Europeans were
herders of cattle and that their attachment
to farming, most likely, does not antedate
their settling down and finding permanent

homelands. Therefore, it makes sense to think that some of them introduced into their sky-oriented pantheon a goddess to whom they could turn for the mating power that would ensure their own fertility as well as that of their flocks.

Contact with non-Indo-European peoples eventually made Aphrodite a composite figure with Mediterranean and Near Eastern features. Yet, one should not lose sight of the fact that even Zeus, the most Indo-European of the Greek gods, eventually was worshipped as *chthonios* (of the earth), and as early as the fifth and fourth centuries, he traveled far enough to be identified with the Egyptian god Ammon and to borrow from him his ram's horns.

The place of composition of this hymn is unknown. Its date seems quite early, somewhere around 700 BC. The story of the love of Anchises and Aphrodite is at least as old as Homer (*Iliad* 2.819–21; 5.311–13). Hesiod also knows the story and mentions it briefly in *Theogony* 1008–10. The brevity of the Homeric and Hesiodic references should not mislead us into thinking that the details of the seduction are altogether new with the poet of the hymn. As we learn from the story of which Demodokos sings in the *Odyssey* (8.266ff.), Aphrodite's amatory escapades caught the fancy of Homer as well. In later Greek literature, Theokritos mentions the episode in 20.34 and Apollodoros gives a somewhat different version in 3.12.2. Given the loveliness of the theme and its possibilities, it is indeed remarkable that it did not become an all-time favorite with the Alexandrians and the Romans (see however, Propertius 2.32 and 35; Nonnus 15.210).

The lay sang by Demodokos in the eighth book of the *Odyssey* is patently humorous and racy. The humor of this hymn is subtle and almost reverential. To begin with, the goddess of our hymn has unique powers over beasts, men, and gods. Such are her powers that not even Zeus can escape them. In fact, this one time he takes revenge by "placing in her soul sweet desire to mate with a mortal" (45–46). In other words, she is acting under some constraint. This is a superbly playful twist by the poet, who prepares the listener for the strangely seductive

maidenly coyness of the goddess when she encounters Anchises. She does not appear to him as a femme fatale or an overpowering goddess, but rather as a young Phrygian princess who has been abducted by Hermes from among other maidens at a dance in honor of the divine maiden Artemis— the emphasis here is on innocence and virginity—and commanded to become the wife of Anchises. She does not tell him that she is unwilling, but she does tell him that she must comply with dire necessity (130). She also insists—good girl that she is—on meeting his parents and his brothers. La noblesse oblige. Anchises is not about to be outdone by an ingénue. He can be just as pious to the wishes of the gods. He boasts that neither man nor god—not even Apollon—can prevent him from obeying the command of Hermes! The listener realizes that this is a double put-on and cannot but think, "Oh, what a way to go!" He undresses her and takes off every last piece of jewelry, as she just stands there with downcast eyes, not lifting a finger to help. Aphrodite pays great attention to her clothing as well as to her jewelry. She stands close to Anchises and she takes care to look very maidenly. She does not reveal her identity. Aphrodite tells Anchises sweet lies and then she infuses passion into his heart. He takes her by the hand. With downcast eyes she crawls into his bed (155–166). The poet goes lightly over the details of their intimacy.

Anchises does his duty and then he promptly falls asleep. Aphrodite is a tease; she cannot wait to break the news to him. So she wakes him up. He gazes upon the goddess as she towers above him in her radiant beauty, and he is seized with surprise and fear for his manhood. The surprise cannot be genuine. After all, he finds out what he already knew, however "unclearly." But the fear is understandable; goddesses have strange ways. However, Aphrodite soothes his anxiety by telling him of the fabulous boy she will bear him and of the fact that there is precedent for what just happened: Zeus took a fancy to Ganymedes, and Eos fell in love with Tithonos. Not only has Anchises not had a bad time of it, but what is more "*non è peccato!*" All this is funny and charming, but it is not impious and picaresque, and this, I think, is to be credited to the unique skill of the composer, who managed to stroll so casually on a veritable literary tightrope. The story about Eos, the dawn goddess who kidnapped Tithonos, fits the occasion.

Throughout hymn 5, Aphrodite is the quintessence of feminine grace. The goddess is modest and self-conscious. When she reaches her temple in Cyprus, she closes the doors, thus protecting herself from undue curiosity.

1. The line is reminiscent of *Odyssey* 1.1. The poet addresses Mnemosyne (Memory), whose aid he understandably needs.

2. Aphrodite is called Kypris (and elsewhere Kyprogenês) either because she was born in Cyprus or because she came to it after her birth. The condition of the Hesiodic passage that refers to Aphrodite's birth (*Theogony* 190–206) hardly permits any sort of dogmatic certainty on the subject.

2–6. The power of Aphrodite, as defined by these lines, extends over man and beast, and is far greater than the one implied by Hesiod in *Theogony* 205–6, where she presides over "maidenly whispers and smiles and tricks, and over sweet delight and honeylike love." The theme of Aphrodite's power is beautifully elaborated by Lucretius (*De Rerum Natura* 1–49), for whom the goddess, essentially, is not only the divine muse invoked to help him in his great undertaking but also the deity governing the *natura rerum* (nature of things). Hesiod tells us that Aphrodite was called Kythereia because as she was floating on the sea, she came close to Kythera, the little island off the coast of the southern Peloponnese (*Theogony* 198).

7–32. This excursus on the chaste character of Athena, Artemis, and Hestia is not only in keeping with the leisurely and digressive pace of the epic but also constitutes a clever foil that brings Aphrodite's amatory nature into full relief.

8–11. The theory that Athena originally was the warlike patroness and palace goddess of the Mycenaean kings (Nilsson 1921) is most likely correct. Her masculine character is also shown by the fact that she was born from the head of Zeus (for Hera's anger, see *Hymn to Apollon* 3.305–62). Behind Athena's aversion to the whole domain of Aphrodite's power may be the idea that sexual love enfeebles men and therefore robs them of vital energy needed in the battlefield.

12–15. Athena was the patroness of crafts and of women's handiwork. In *Odyssey* 6.233, we find her as patron goddess of goldsmiths, and in Athens the smiths held a festival (the *Chalkeia*) in her honor. The epithet Erganê ("lady-worker") also attests to her connection with craft and handiwork. Hesiod calls the plow-builder a servant of Athena.

21–32. Hestia was the first child born to Rhea and Kronos, Demeter was second, and Hera third (Hesiod *Theogony* 454). As the oldest child, Hestia was first to be swallowed and last to be disgorged by her father (*Theogony* 495ff.). In a sense, she was also the youngest. She was the first and last deity to whom libations were poured at a feast. Mythology never made much of Apollon's and Poseidon's wooing of Hestia, perhaps because she never became truly anthropomorphic. Furthermore, whenever she was thought of in human form, she was considered a virgin. This last concept of the goddess as a virgin is also supported by the fact that the priestesses of her etymologically cognate divine counterpart in Rome, Vesta, had to remain chaste during their service to the temple. Line 30 is consonant with Homeric practice, since the hearth was in the center of the *megaron* (the main hall in a palace or a large house). The claim that Hestia "for all mortals . . . is of all gods the most venerated" (32) needs some qualification. Surely Hestia was not more venerated than Zeus. The poet must mean that, where life from day to day was concerned, much of the domestic piety was lavished on Hestia, who presided over the *lares* and *penates* (the domestic divinities) of the pagan household. Hesiod has only one curious injunction with regard to Hestia: a man should avoid showing his genitals to Hestia if they are besprinkled with semen (*Works and Days* 733–34). The virginal nature of the goddess may have been the reason why such unsightly testimony of copulation might be repugnant to her and therefore offensive.

34–35. For the power of Aphrodite and her ability to charm both gods and mortals, see Sophocles *Antigone* 788–90 and Euripides *Hippolytos* 1264–75.

36–52. For Zeus's susceptibility to Aphrodite's power and his impressive extramarital adventures, see Hesiod *Theogony* 886ff. Zeus's own immodest account is found in *Iliad* 14.312ff.

58–64. The cult of Aphrodite was widespread in Cyprus. At the end of the poem, Aphrodite is called "queen of cultivated Cyprus." There was a beautiful temple dedicated to her in Paphos. So she came to this temple, where the Graces bathed her and anointed her with fragrant and immortal divine oil. In the *Iliad* and the *Odyssey* Aphrodite is called "golden" or "she of the golden-throne." Her bracelets are golden. She is decked out with gold and from the breasts of the goddess emanates a light like that of the moon (89–90). In the *Iliad*, the epithet "of the golden throne" qualifies Hera (1.611) and Artemis (9.529). In *Odyssey* 19.319, this epithet qualifies Eos (Dawn) and other goddesses as well.

70–74. Wild beasts fawn on Odysseus's men as they approach the palace of Kirke (*Odyssey* 10.211–19). For wild animals fawning on approaching goddesses, see Apollonios Rhodios 1.1144; 3.878; 4.672. For Aphrodite's effect on the animal kingdom, see Lucretius's highly poetical account in *De Rerum Natura* 10–20.

81–85. The idea here is that however much a goddess may change, she is still divine enough to look extraordinary. Thus, in the *Hymn to Demeter,* even though the goddess is disguised as an old woman when she enters the palace of Keleos, her head touches the roof beam, and the doors are filled with divine radiance (2.184–86). Yet, no one recognizes her because "gods are not easily seen by men" (2.111).

86–90. The passion of the goddess was extraordinary. It set, as it were, her robe on fire. The robe that is "more brilliant than gleaming fire" is a poetic metaphor for the glowing heat of erotic passion. Ladies change robes, and their passions come and go, but the attributes that are part of the substance of a divinity are of a higher order—they belong to their essence. The lunar radiance emanating from Aphrodite's breasts is soft and feminine. Moonlight is soft and feminine, and "moon" in Greek ("selênê") is feminine in terms of both

personification and grammatical gender. The light that emblazons the goddess so strikingly in this scene is a feminine light.

92–106. Anchises is far more perceptive than the womenfolk at the palace of Keleos; he knows that Aphrodite is a goddess.

107–42. We may conjecture that this is the same Otreus, who, in the *Iliad,* together with Mygdon, is king of the Phrygians (3.182–90). The account Aphrodite gives in these lines is full of sweet lies. Greek culture considered lying under certain circumstances an absolute necessity. In the *Odyssey,* Odysseus, posing as a stranger, lies to Penelope. Of course, he lies to the Cyclops. He tells the cannibal that his name is Nobody. In the *Hymn to Demeter*, the goddess lies to the daughters of Keleos when she is asked to reveal her identity.

113–16. This is the first passage in which the difference between languages is recognized. Homer made no attempt to present the speech of the non-Greeks of his epics in such a way as to show us that they were speakers of different languages. Yet he knew that languages other than Greek were spoken by the Asians of the Trojan host (*Iliad* 2.808; 4.437) and that the Carians spoke a barbarian language.

126–42. Aphrodite's plea is both ingenious and ingenuous. She offers herself to Anchises in marriage as a nobly dowered young bride, who wants all proprieties observed and who does this out of pious compliance with divine will. Her attitude mirrors the typically Greek attitude expressed in the phrase "theós pou" ("somehow a god did it"). Aphrodite goes over every detail of a formal marriage. She asks Anchises to present her to his family as a proper bride and to send a messenger to the Phrygians to tell her mother and father about all this. In return, they will send gold to him and many woven garments, splendid gifts that he must accept. After he does all this, he must prepare a wedding feast such as would be honored both by men and by immortal gods.

145–54. Anchises's answer is rather humorous, since he really turns compelling necessity to virtue and piety. In truth, he is so inflamed by the beauty of the young woman that he is willing to defy the arrows of Apollon and even to die for the pleasure of going to bed with her. For the irrational passion that Aphrodite can inspire, see *Odyssey* 8.335–42.

161–65. An inferior poet would have Aphrodite undress herself. But we must remember that she is a coy and untouched young maiden, whose feigned passivity emboldens the resolve of the young shepherd.

168–75. Aphrodite waited until the evening. She then poured sweet sleep over Anchises. She changed to even more beautiful clothes and stood by the bed. Her head touched the roof beam as her cheeks radiated with divine beauty.

172–75. The lines are reminiscent of the *Hymn to Demeter* (2.188–90). The earlier magnificent epiphany of Aphrodite, which is so poetically described in lines 84–90, was not perceived by Anchises for what it was. He was dazed, driven blind as it were. He succumbed to the onslaught of feminine power on a divine scale, and he slept with his divine visitor, but still he did not realize that he lay in love next to the goddess of love. The epiphany described in lines 2.172–75 is simpler, easier to perceive. Here we see how radiance migrated to the cheeks of the goddess after her passion was stilled and succeeded by bashfulness.

180–90. We might think that it is a general apprehension in the presence of the divine that seizes Anchises, but he has not simply seen Aphrodite; he has slept with her. In modern Greek folklore, men who have been seduced into intercourse with a Nereid (a fairy) usually lose their wits and betimes their manhood. In the epic of Gilgamesh, the hero rejects the advances made by Ishtar because he knows that the lovers of this Eastern Aphrodite come to no good end. Kalypso does not harm Odysseus, but obviously Kirke has the power to deprive Odysseus of his manliness (*Odyssey* 10.301). Perhaps Anchises fears that once the goddess has taken her pleasure with him, she will make him impotent to make sure that no mortal woman can ever boast of having lain with the favorite of Aphrodite.

196–99. The poet derives the name from "ainós" ("dread" or "awesome") and adds the usual folk etymology. In the *Iliad*, Aineias (obviously derived from "ainós") is one of the foremost and bravest Trojan leaders,

frequently mentioned side by side with Hector (17.513).

202–17. In the *Iliad*, it is the other gods who abduct Ganymedes (20.230–35). For the fabulous horses of Tros, see *Iliad* 5.265–72.

218–38. Here the myth of Eos and Tithonos is fully developed. Homer knows Tithonos as a consort of Eos but mentions nothing about Eos's thoughtless request that reduced her lover to the unending misery of eternal life accompanied by the ravages of progressive old age (see *Iliad* 11.1; 20.237). Sappho (frag. 58 LP) and Mimnermos (frag. 12 West) follow the tradition of the Homeric hymn. The story that Tithonos was eventually turned into a cicada is much later.

260. Nymphs lived long but were not immortal.

262. Seilenoi are often portrayed as lovers of nymphs on Greek vases.

264–72. This belief must go back to an even more primitive animistic concept according to which the tree was hardly distinguished from its spirit. Later, the spirit detached itself, became anthropomorphic, and lived an existence that was independent as long as the tree lived but came to an end when the tree died. For a scholarly reference to this idea, see Gantz (1993); Kallimachos *Hymn to Hermes* 4.83–5; and Ovid *Metamorphoses* 8.738–878.

276–77. Herodotos tells us that Persian children were not seen by their fathers before the age of five, and that up to that time they were always kept in the company of the ladies who looked after them (1.136).

278–85. Aphrodite instructs Anchises to send his infant son to Ilion and to say that the child's mother is a nymph. She asks him not to reveal her identity.

286–93. Anchises is told that if he names the goddess as the child's mother, Zeus will strike him dead with his thunderbolt. Obviously, the goddess does not want people to know that she slept with a mortal.

6 : To Aphrodite

The date and place of composition for this shorter hymn to Aphrodite are unknown. The hymn may not be very late, but it is not very early either. The poet may have been a Cypriot.

Hymn 6 is a magnificat to the beauty of the goddess. The Horae are dressing Aphrodite and are preparing to present her to the gods. The details indicate that Aphrodite is ready for this occasion, the way a bride is prepared for presentation to her new family. This idea is supported by lines 16–17, where we are told that each one of the male gods, upon seeing her, wishes that he could take her home as his wedded wife. At the end of the poem, epithets describing the loveliness of Aphrodite are followed by the poet's prayer for victory in the contest.

Aphrodite's cults were numerous. Hence, a wide range of epithets is applied to her various functions. Her power over the black earth reminds us of her connection with fertility. In Corinth, she is a protectress of prostitutes. Elsewhere, as Aphrodite Pelagia, she helps sailors. Some extremely rare statues show her armed and even bearded. In Ancient India a young woman of marriageable age could choose one of several suitors to be her husband. Almost always, the chosen suitor had to demonstrate extraordinary skill in a contest. This practice is called "swayamvara" in Sanskrit. Draupadi and Damayanti, both of whom are prominent in the epic *Mahabharata*, choose their husbands in this fashion. Hymn 6 has elements of this serious matrimonial action (see Hunter 2005; Ormand 2014). One would expect Aphrodite to be married to Ares, the handsome god of war. Instead, she is married to Hephaistos, a strange and ungainly god. The two are a very odd couple, which can be explained only in terms of comedy.

1–5. In Homer, Aphrodite is the daughter of Zeus and Dionê (*Iliad* 5.312). The poet of this hymn obviously follows Hesiod's account, which has Aphrodite born in the sea from the foam that surrounded the genitals of Ouranos. In fact, Hesiod believes that the name of the goddess is derived from the word "aphros," the "foam" in which she was nourished (*Theogony* 173–206).

5–14. The Horae and the Graces (Charites) are almost identical. In Hesiod, the Horae collaborate with the Graces to adorn and deck out Pandora (*Works and Days* 69–82). According to Hesiod, they are three in number: Eunomia, Dikê, and Eirenê (*Theogony*

900). In Attica, too, their number was three (Thallô, Karpô, and Auxô), but in Hellenistic times they were identified with the four seasons. The vacillation in classical art between two and three Horae may mirror the Indo-European concept of the year as divided into a cold and warm period (winter-summer) as well as into three distinct seasons: winter, spring, and summer.

7 : To Dionysos

Some scholars have seen less skill and grace in this hymn, and they have tried to place it either in Alexandrian times or, worse yet, within our own first centuries AD. Others have found a dithyrambic quality in it. I take this to mean that they have felt some resemblance between this hymn and the dithyrambic poems by Bacchylides. These assumptions are erroneous, especially as they fail to appreciate the fact that there is not one single thing in this hymn that bespeaks either artlessness or a late date. Further, our knowledge of dithyrambic poetry is so meager that it is rather otiose to venture into any comparisons. The hymn treats an episode out of the god's life and evolves along the lines of a reasonably common thematic motif, which is based on the idea that most men are blind to the presence of divinity and that gods are forced to resort to miracles in order to manifest their divine nature. I suppose it is the quick and almost cinematic pace of the poet that has caught critics by surprise. Digression and formulaic repetition are absent. But the poet should not be castigated for his economy of literary devices. He has a moral to teach, and he does it by painting a very lovely and telling picture with a few slightly nervous but powerful strokes. As for the date, there is no good reason to believe that the hymn is later than the sixth century.

Hymn 7 is full of action and exciting imagery. This has not escaped the attention of vase painters. Especially popular with them was the vine with its almost sensual clusters of grapes (38–41). Another favorite was the image of sailors leaping into the sea and being transformed into dolphins (50–53).

We have a story here. Dionysos showed up at a lonely beach. His black hair rippled over his shoulders, which were covered by a purple cloak. Soon Tyrsenian pirates swiftly crossed the wine-dark sea. It was evil fate that drove them there. They thought that Dionysos was a wealthy prince. So, they grabbed him and wanted to put him in shackles. They did so, but the shackles came loose and the withes fell off his hands and feet. Dionysos simply sat there smiling. Miracles started taking place. A vine climbed up the mast. Fragrant wine was flowing everywhere. Suddenly, the dark-haired young man changed shapes. He first became a lion and then a bear. The Hyperboreans are mentioned in line 29 as a probable destination of the stranger. Everything that happens testifies to the presence of Dionysos.

Survivals are always very interesting. The central theme of hymn 7 presents the ability of Dionysos to set himself free and to punish those who have tried to capture him. So then he is the god of utter freedom and release. Saint Eleutherios, born in Rome, was martyred sometime during the second half of the second century AD. In the Greek Orthodox Church, he is venerated especially as protector of pregnant women and also as a saint who grants freedom to those who are imprisoned. In both of these capacities he may have inherited functions of Dionysos Eleutherios. If this is true, we have here one more instance of a Christian saint assuming aspects of a non-Christian divinity.

1. See note 4 on hymn 1 to Dionysos.

2ff. The story of the capture of Dionysos by pirates is found in several other literary sources: Euripides *Cyclops* 11ff.; Apollodoros 3.5.3; Ovid *Metamorphoses* 3.582–691; and Hyginus *Fabula* 134. A modified version of the story forms the theme on the choregic monument of Lysikrates (334 BC).

3–6. Except for the cloak on his shoulders, the youthful Dionysos resembles an archaic Greek *kouros* (athletic young man) and is very different from the blond, curly-haired, and seductive Dionysos of Euripides's *Bacchae* 233–41. The Aristophanic caricature of the god in the *Frogs* is also a far cry from the robust and virile youth of our hymn here.

8. There are other stories in which the Tyrsenians are pirates (see the story of the rape of the Athenian women at Brauron in Herodotos 6.138). Although writers of the fifth

century BC used the names "Tyrsenians" and "Pelasgians" to refer to the pre-Hellenic world, there is nothing eliminating the possibility that the composer of the hymn might have the better-known Etruscans (also called Tyrsenians) in mind, whose piratic raids must have been familiar to the Greeks in early historic times.

13. For the power of Dionysos to undo shackles forced on him, see Euripides *Bacchae* 447, 498, 616ff.

19–20. The point is that Dionysos looks like a god. He certainly does not look like fair-haired Apollon or like the bearded Zeus and Poseidon, but gods frequently changed their form, and in addition to this, the helmsman's awe would make attention to such obvious differences less effective.

29. The Hyperboreans were a northerly legendary folk visited by Apollon part of the year. Homer does not know of them, and they occur first in Hesiod fragment 209 (see Alkaios A.I(c) LP, 1.1 Loeb; Pindar *Olympian Ode* 3.16 and *Pythian* 10.30 ff.; Herodotos 4.32).

35–44. These lines are reminiscent of the famous vase of Exekias, now one of the precious possessions of the Antike Kunstsammlung in Munich.

44. Dionysos is frequently transformed into a lion (see Euripides's *Bacchae*).

53. In the Exekias vase, Dionysos is represented as a bearded regal man, majestically reclining on a boat from whose mast and rigging vine branches and grapes are hanging. Dolphins swim about the boat. Although it cannot be maintained that these dolphins are the transformed pirates of our story here, a conflation of motifs is by no means impossible.

8 : To Ares

Both the accumulation of epithets in the beginning and the astrological character of the hymn make it more than probable that we are dealing with a late—perhaps Alexandrian or even later—poem. So odd seems the inclusion of this poem among the Homeric Hymns that scholars are at a loss for an explanation.

Ares looks like an afterthought in the construction of the divine Olympian hierarchy. He does not seem to have an analogue in the traditions of the Germanic peoples. The root "ari" is found in Greek "aristos," Persian "ariya," and so on. Everywhere it basically means "masculine" and, hence, "powerful" and "superior." The term "Aryans," meaning "superior people," goes back to this prolific Indo-European root. Temples to Ares are not frequent. Yet, they do exist especially in the Peloponnese and Crete.

Homer has nothing good to say about war. Even as a god, Ares is quite a bit of a clown. He invades the domestic space of Hephaistos to sleep with his wife, Aphrodite (*Odyssey* 8.265–332). Details for ritual in the cults of Ares are missing, and there are not so many cults honoring the god of war anyway. He is frequently identified with Enyalios, another war god. In lines 191–97 of the poem *Shield* (*Aspis*), falsely attributed to Hesiod, Ares is presented very vividly as a blood-curdling god (Athanassakis 2004a):

> Carrying the spoils of war,
> he rode on a chariot
> and, sharp-tipped spear in hand,
> he gave orders to foot soldiers.
> He was coated with crimson blood,
> as if he were slaying living men.
> And next to him stood
> Panic and Fear, yearning
> to leap amid the battling ranks.

4. Nikê (Victory) is the daughter of Styx and Pallas (Hesiod *Theogony* 383–84). Ares begets Victory only in a symbolic manner. Themis is a Titan and the daughter of Ouranos and Gaia (*Theogony* 135). She is also Zeus's second consort, and as such she gives birth to the Horae and Moirai. Her name means "established custom," "law," and "justice," and she eventually becomes an abstraction. Here "helper of Themis" surely means "succorer of Justice."

5. In Greek, the words "kakos" ("bad," "cowardly") and "kalos" ("noble," "brave") are antonyms. Since the antonym of bad is good, Ares, who is patron of the good, is perforce patron and leader of the just. In cult, Ares was not linked with the concept of justice or law, and in the *Iliad* there is no sentiment that the god of war chooses to fight on the side of the just. The ultimate meaning of the line must be that those who support law and order may resort to war,

hoping to enlist the support of Ares, who, as a god, should be expected to refuse his support to the lawless and the unruly. After all, in Homer, kingly authority comes from Zeus, and Ares should come to the aid of the side favored by his father.

6–8. Here the poet switches from Ares the god to Ares the planet (Mars). The peculiar redness of Mars was known to the ancients, and astronomical literature refers to the planet with several adjectives that contain the word "pyr" ("fire") as their base. Ares is carried "above the third heavenly arch" because in all Greek astronomical systems he occupied the third planetary zone, counting from the one farthest from the earth (counting from the one closest to the earth, his zone was fifth).

9–15. Although general astrological doctrine taught that the influence of Mars was untoward and evil, I very much doubt that this line is euphemistic. The composer of the hymn does not distinguish between Ares the god and Ares the planet. He bypasses astrological doctrine and dwells on those qualities of the god that are potentially positive.

16. Since Ares controls war, he also controls peace (see Orphic hymn 65.6).

9 : To Artemis

There should be little doubt as to the place of origin of the hymn. It must be Asia Minor rather than the Aegean or mainland Greece. The date need not be late. Like so many of the very short hymns, this one is a mere appeal to the goddess, perhaps even a brief introduction to something else. Artemis is a very important and very popular goddess. In *Odyssey* 20.61–90, Penelope prays to her. In Sparta she is worshipped as Artemis Orthia. The festival in honor of Artemis in Sparta was a splendid event. In a poem by Alkman, choruses of young and beautiful Spartan women compete in a race to reach the temple of the goddess before dawn. As Artemis Brauronia in Attica, she is protectress of very young girls who spend time in her temple to be introduced to the rituals of the goddess. The little girls, most likely ages six to twelve, become *arktoi* (bears) in rituals that introduce them to social and religious aspects of their premenstrual age. These very young girls wore a special crocus-colored robe for the occasion (Arist. *Lysistrata* 641–646). All this rich lore does not appear in this hymn, which is almost a mere salutation to the goddess. A plethora of inscriptions unearthed by excavations in the archaeological site of Brauron are awaiting proper archaeological attention. Only a few inscriptions are displayed in the museum at Brauron.

3. Although in art and literature Artemis is sometimes connected with horses, it is usually stags and deer that she drives (so on the frieze of Apollon's temple at Bassai). The river Meles flowed near Smyrna, and, according to one story, Homer was born on its banks and composed his poems in a nearby grotto (Paus. 7.5.6). The river is represented on coins of Smyrna.

4. Smyrna is mentioned because the goddess would naturally pay a quick visit to her temple there (see Quintus Smyrnaeus 7.310). It is not surprising that Artemis of Ephesos is not mentioned in this hymn. Most likely the occasion for the present short composition was a festival at Smyrna, so it was not proper to praise another city.

5. For Klaros, see note on *Hymn to Apollon* 3.30–44.

10 : To Aphrodite

This brief prelude may have been composed by a patriotic Cypriot. Its brevity does not allow us to make any safe pronouncements on its date. The poet highlights the sweetness of Aphrodite's gifts and the irresistible desire her smile instills in people. One may look for this smile on statues of the goddess that come especially from classical times. The smile is a blend of erotic desire and reverence for the power of the goddess of love. (See Hesiod *Theogony* 201–206; Mimnermos, frag. 1.3 West; and especially Sappho, frag. 1.13–14 LP.

11 : To Athena

The joint appeal to Athena and Ares may be a case of mere metonymy. "She and Ares" may simply mean war-like Athena. In so many ways, Ares stands to Athena as an attribute. In hymn 11 Athena is praised as a protectress of armies going to war and returning from it as well.

This brief hymn has the basic characteristics of a prelude, and it may be quite early.

Athena is called "defender of cities" in *Iliad* 6.305. Her usual title is *poliouchos* (holder or keeper of cities). Although Athena and Ares were rarely worshipped or invoked together, instances to the contrary are not wanting (see Paus. 5.15.6 and 1.8.5; also Pindar *Nemean Ode* 10.84).

Athena not only protects cities under siege, but she also "sacks" cities. Her role as defender of cities was taken over by the Holy Virgin, who in the famous hymn (to be precise, it is a *kontakion*, a church hymn with formal structure) of the Greek Orthodox Church composed by Romanos Melodos in Constantinople after the "rebellion of Nika" in 532, is called "defending general." In the fervid prayers to the Mother of Christ, preceding the holiday of the dormition, August 15, Panagia, the All-Holy Mother of Jesus, is called "a weapon and a fortress that cannot be sacked." All this is very close to Athena's role in antiquity as a protectress of cities. The Holy Virgin, in addition to being, like Athena, a virgin, has also assumed many of the functions of Athena. The birth of the goddess from the head of Zeus is described by Hesiod in *Theogony* 886–900.

12 : To Hera

Hera, daughter of Kronos and Rhea, is a queenly presence among the gods. The epithet "golden-throned" in the first line, which Hera shares with Aphrodite of Sappho 1.13, emphasizes the elevated status of the wife of Zeus. Hera, also a sister of Zeus, is the prototype of a jealous wife who persecutes all women favored by Zeus. Marriage within the family may have an anthropological analogue in very primitive or simply endogamous peoples. The jealous and vindictive side of Hera is suppressed entirely in this hymn. This makes sense, since the occasion must have been festive. As there is no farewell to the deity addressed—and this, incidentally, is the only example of its kind in the entire collection—these lines may indeed be the introduction to a longer poem.

In Hesiod *Theogony* 12, Hera "walks in golden sandals," and in *Theogony* 433–34 "golden-sandaled" Hera is the daughter of Kronos and Rhea. See also *poikilothronos* (of the intricate or variegated throne), said of Aphrodite in Sappho, frag. 1.1 LP.

The cult of Hera and her majestic temple as well as the equally grand temple to Zeus built in the Olympiad of 476 BC would be reason enough for a poet to make specific reference to Olympia. Also the Iliadic Zeus, and especially Zeus Dodonaios to whom Achilles prays in the *Iliad* (16.233), would also be a good reason for the composer of this short poem to devote to Zeus at least a litany of the epithets that point to some of his major accomplishments, such as the defeat of the Titans and of Typhoeus.

In the fourteenth book of the *Iliad*, in a very well-known episode, a very cunning and very conspiratory Hera enlists the help of Hypnos (Sleep) to put Zeus to sleep and thus remove him from active participation in the course of events (14.161–359).

A monumental temple to Hera was built at Olympia in the sixth century BC. Both the geographic position of this temple, its proximity to the cult of Zeus, as well as the celebration of the Olympic games every four years made this temple to Hera unique. Yet, there is no mention of it here. We have no hint of plot and no allusion to some great moment in the mythology of the goddess.

13 : To Demeter

It is not clear what the function of such a short piece would be. It is a salutatory address lacking any luster or any reference to cultic practices. This piece is too short to have had any significance. Perhaps it was detached by mistake from a longer hymn.

14 : To the Mother of the Gods

The present hymn does contain orgiastic features and is comparable to the much later Orphic hymn 27, also devoted to the mother of the gods. Although it is quite plausible that the hymn was composed as a prelude to recitation at some sort of orgiastic worship, there is no indication that it is Orphic or late. In fact, its stark directness and lack of mythological elaboration make it definitely pre-Alexandrian.

1–2. The "Mother of the Gods" is frequently identified with Rhea, as for example in Orphic hymn 14 (see also Orphic hymn 27) where she is simply called "Mother of the Gods." That Rhea is thought of as mother of the gods is clear from *Iliad* 15.187 and Hesiod *Theogony* 453, 625, and 634. By "Muse," the poet may have meant either all of the Muses collectively or just one, perhaps Kalliope (see Hesiod *Theogony* 1–115).

3. The line reminds us of the worship of Kybele. Rattles, drums, and the sounds of wild flutes leave no doubt as to the identity of the goddess. Present also is the worship of Dionysos. See *Bacchae* 155–156.

4–5. The lion is the most devoted companion of the Mother of the Gods in poetry, vase painting, and sculpture. The presence of wolves and lions howling in the wilds suggests the pre-Hellenic Potnia Theron (Mistress of Animals).

15 : To Lion-Hearted Herakles

So Panhellenic was the worship of Herakles that there is no good reason to ascribe the hymn to a Theban rhapsode. Most likely, it is pre-Alexandrian and may perhaps have been composed in quite early times. This hymn gives no specifics about the labors of Herakles. We are simply told that Herakles wandered over the vast earth as well as over the sea, executing missions given to him by Eurystheus, king of the Argolid. *Odyssey* 11.600–640 may be read with great profit. These lines offer us information about the labors of Herakles as well as about the duality of his nature. Indeed, the human essence of Herakles, his human soul, ends up in Hades while the immortal part of him is elevated to Olympian status.

1–3. For the circumstances of the birth of Herakles, see pseudo-Hesiodic *Shield* 1–54.

4–8. Relevant to this brief hymn are Hesiod's *Theogony* lines 950–55, which describe the glorious career of Herakles. Pindar in *Nemean Ode* 1.37–43 describes how Hera, jealous of Alkmene, mother of Herakles, tried to kill him.

9. The phrase I have translated "Grant me virtue and happiness" is both conventional and formulaic. However, to pray to Herakles for virtue, especially manly virtue, which is most likely meant here, is appropriate. Although "olbos" ("happiness") may also mean "wealth"—and although among the Greeks of southern Italy, Herakles was

connected with commerce—one should
cautiously refrain from taking the formula
too literally.

We note here that for the composer of
this hymn, Herakles was the son of Zeus,
born to him by beautiful Alkmene, wife of
Amphitryon. Herakles was a hero eventually raised to divine status. His marriage to
Hebe, daughter of Hera and Zeus and cupbearer of the gods, secures him a position
among the Olympian gods. In addition to
being a son of Zeus, he eventually becomes
Zeus's son-in law as well. Hymn 15 makes
no mention of Amphitryon, husband of
Alkmene, nor of Iphikles, the human twin
brother of Herakles. The omission seems
deliberate.

16 : To Asklepios

Apollon became enamored of Koronis,
daughter of Phlegyas. The eventual union
resulted in the birth of Asklepios. Many
later elaborations are attributed to mythographers and do not seem essential. In the
Iliad, Asklepios is a "blameless physician"
(11.518). The two physicians of the Greeks
at Troy, Machaon and Podaleirios, are his
sons (2.732). Although his worship spread
far and wide in the Hellenic world, it seems
to have originated in Thessalian Trikka. In
Hellenistic times, Epidauros and Kos boasted the most splendid temples to Asklepios.
Originally, Asklepios must have been a hero
physician who was eventually elevated to
divine status. The present hymn does not
emphasize the Thessalian origin. As for
the date, the sixth century is a good guess.
There is no mention of a specific cult of
Asklepios, not even of his cult at Epidauros.
The hymn may simply be a short prayer
or, more precisely, an invocation. For the
story of the birth of Asklepios, see Hesiod
Theogony 50; Pindar *Pythian Ode* 3.1–53; and
Ovid *Metamorphoses* 2.600–634.

17 : To the Dioskouroi

The Dioskouroi were twin sons of Zeus and
Leda, daughter of King Thestios of Pleuron
in Aitolia (see notes to the longer hymn 33
to the Dioskouroi). Through Leda, they
are also Helen's brothers. Many significant
details of Greek mythology were invented
in the effort to construct genealogical trees,
usually links to heroic and even divine
status.

18 : To Hermes

Hymn 18 mentions some of the essential
functions of the god. He rules over Arcadia,
rich in flocks. He is a messenger of the gods
who grants flocks their luxuriant hair and
who also helps shepherds by breaking paths
through thick growth. Some of the functions of Hermes were eventually distributed
to Christian saints. An example is offered by
Saint Mamas who was born in the middle of
the third century AD and was martyred in
Rome toward the end of the third century.
He protects shepherds and flocks. His feast
day on September 2 is an occasion for great
celebration. Many lambs offered by pilgrims
are slaughtered, literally sacrificed, in honor
of Saint Mamas. The saint's name poses
etymological problems.

12. The word I have translated as "giver of
things graceful" is "charidôtês," which more
literally means "giver of grace" (see *Odyssey*
15.319–20). For a cult of Hermes Charidôtês
see Plutarch *Moralia* 503. Some of the notes
on the longer *Hymn to Hermes* (hymn 4)
are also applicable to this shorter version.
Hymn 18 seems to be an abstraction of
hymn 4 and as such a more convenient
prelude. Both hymns may be from the same
century.

19 : To Pan

Apollon, the handsome and luminous god,
decided to go to Arcadia, where he fell in
love with Dryope, the beautiful daughter
of Dryops. It could not be otherwise, since
beautiful young women find strangers
fascinating. The child born of this marriage
was a monstrosity as he had goat's feet
and horns and also was very boisterous.
Many examples of his weird appearance are
found in vase paintings. When his mother
saw him, she was frightened and ran away.
Despite the very peculiar appearance of the
child, Hermes took him to Olympos, to
present him to the gods. All were delighted,
especially Dionysos. Pan is a lecherous god
who instills libido in gods and men. His
looks and behavior link him with male goats
when they rut at the end of summer and
beginning of fall. At this time of the year,

male goats explode with hormonal energy.
They wander from flock to flock, and when
they return to their own flock, they are
entirely spent. There are some tempting
etymologies about the word "Pan" but none
of them is entirely secure. Pan plays sweet
music on the pipes he himself invented. He
is the only god who dies. Usually Pan dwells
in caves, and there is a cave devoted to Pan
close to the cave of the Muses and close
to the Athenian Acropolis. Pan's looks are
monstrous, and in later times he is associated with Satan. In a beautiful icon signed by
Lazaros the iconographer, and dated 1457,
Saint Marina is about to strike Satan, who is
winged and sports two horns.

    Art and literature before the sixth centu-
ry BC take little or no notice of Pan. Indeed,
in the first half of the millennium, Pan
seems to have remained a wantonly sportive
and gamboling god of the Arcadian woodlands. Before 490 BC, there was no shrine
to Pan in Athens, and it seems that his cult
was introduced as a result of his decisive
intervention on behalf of the Athenians in
the struggle against the Persians, whom he
struck with panic and terror (Herodotos
6.105). It is highly unlikely that the hymn
antedates the date of the battle of Marathon (490 BC) and equally unlikely that it
is Alexandrian. The fifth century seems a
reasonable date, and Attica a probable place
of composition.

2. These epithets are well attested in literature
and art.

3–7. The domain of Pan was in the hills of
Arcadia, among which Lykaion, Kyllene,
Mainalos, and Parthenion were especially
sacred to him.

12–16. Much as Artemis, the goddess of woodlands, goat-footed Pan is both a hunter and
a patron of hunters. One of the scholia on
Theokritos 7.106 tells us that Arcadian boys
struck images of Pan with squills, lily-like
plants, whenever hunting was not success-
ful.

17–18. The bird is the nightingale, and the
lines are vaguely reminiscent of Sophocles
Oedipus Coloneus 670–79.

19–24. For Pan and the nymphs, see W. H.
Roscher, *Lexikon* 3.1390 and 1420.

22–26. Pan's reputation as a dancer is commonplace in classical literature (see Sophocles

Ajax 696; Aeschylus *Persians* 450). For an
instructive overview of Greek dance in
antiquity, see Lawler (1978).

31. For the secrecy that surrounds the birth of
Hermes, father of Pan, see *Hymn to Hermes*
4.1–9.

34. The nymph in question is Dryope, daughter of Dryops, and originally perhaps an oak
spirit.

35–39. For another version of the story of
Dryope, see Stephanus Byzantinus s.v.
"Dryope" and Ovid *Metamorphoses* 9.325ff.

42. Coins from Messana and Rhegium show
the hare as a symbol of Pan.

46. On the connection between Pan and Dionysos, see Lucian *Dialogue of the Gods* 22.3.

47. This is good folk etymology. The root "pa"
seen in the Greek "paomai" ("to acquire"),
or "passomai" in the future tense, and the
Latin "pascor" ("to feed, graze on") is a
more likely linguistic ancestor of Pan.

20 : To Hephaistos

Hephaistos is a working god and a very
skilled craftsman. He hammers metal into
beautiful shape. In book 18 of the *Iliad*, he
crafts the great shield of Achilles, which is
a map of the whole world surrounded by
the stream of Okeanos. He is assisted in
his work by very willing and very attractive
robot girls. These fabulous assistants have
intelligence, voice, and also strength in
them (18.417–20). By the way, these are the
first robots ever mentioned in the history of
humankind. Hephaistos is the only god who
has a physical defect. He is limping. Some of
the heroes are marked by a physical defect.
Odysseus has a scar on his knee. Achilles
has a vulnerable heel. In Norse religion,
Odin is one-eyed.

2. The concept of Hephaistos and Athena
as joint patrons of handicraft is found in
Homer (*Odyssey* 6.233). It is interesting that
it is Hephaistos who, at the behest of Zeus,
creates Pandora out of earth and water, and
that Athena teaches her the art of weaving
(Hesiod *Works and Days* 59–64). Although
there are indications that Hephaistos was
worshipped in other parts of the Hellenic
world, Athens and Lemnos were the two
most prominent centers of his worship.
In connection with the Lemnian cult of
Hephaistos, about which we know very

little, we may speculate that it must have been old. In Athens, Hephaistos and Athena were worshipped together as patrons of arts and crafts (see Plato *Kritias* 109c, 112b; *Laws* 920d; *Protagoras* 321d). For their place in Orphic belief, see Kern (1922, frag. 178, 179). As with the preceding hymn, Athens and the fifth century seem to be the probable place and date of composition.

In the *Iliad,* we are told that the angered Zeus casts Hephaistos out of the divine threshold. After a full day's journey through the air, the hapless lands on Lemnos, where the legendary Sinties look after him (*Iliad* 1.586–94). In the eighth book of the *Odyssey,* Ares sleeps with Aphrodite, wife of Hephaistos. However, Hephaistos traps him in a snare and makes a laughingstock of him before the gods. So, in this union of the beautiful and the not so beautiful, the intent may be comedy, through the matching of opposites.

21 : To Apollon

The image of a swan singing of Apollon as it breasts an eddying stream is very beautiful. The idea that the swan song comes from the quivering of the swan's wings is perhaps taken from Hesiod *Works and Days* 582–584 where the chirping of the cicadas is produced by a quivering of their wings. In fact, the chirping sound of a cicada is produced by the vibration of its thorax. This hymn is not a cento and does not stand in a derivative relationship to hymn 3. It is a clever rhapsodic prelude of unknown date and place of composition.

1–2. Peculiar though it may seem to us, the ancients believed that a musical sound was produced by the flapping of the swan's wings (see Anacreontea 60.10 Bergk *PLG*).

3. Peneios is the lovely Thessalian river that flows into the Thermaic gulf.

4. Hesiod is commanded to sing of the Muses first and last (*Theogony* 34).

22 : To Poseidon

Poseidon is lord of the earth as well as lord of the waters. Primarily he is master of the seas. The root "dan" is found in many words that are connected with water. Danaos, Danube, perhaps Donn, and Dnieper are all names of great rivers. Yet some schol-ars suggest, and they may be right, that the root "da," related to "ga" and meaning "earth" may be the origin of the name. That Poseidon is lord of Helikon seems like a bit of an oddity. Perhaps there was a temple or a shrine devoted to him somewhere in Helikon. Perhaps, again, inlanders needed his protection when they took to perilous seas. His special relationship with horses may be a poetic metaphor: the rolling waves of the sea might seem like manes of running horses. The magnificent temple devoted to Poseidon at Sounion is emblematic of the importance of the naval power for Athens. Carved on one of the pillars of the temple is the name of none other than Lord Byron. Although the hymn seems like a short prayer to the god of the sea, there is no formal criterion that separates it from the shorter preludes. Date and place of composition are unknown.

2. The line is addressed to Poseidon as god of earthquakes and of the sea. In the Homeric epics, Poseidon is called *enosichthôn* ("earthshaker") in numerous passages, but he considered himself *homotimos* (of equal honor) to Zeus and Hades, because when the tripartite division was made, he was given the sea as his domain (*Iliad* 15.186–91).

3. There is surely a connection between the assertion made in this line and the cult epithet Helikônios under which Poseidon was worshipped by the various Ionian states. Despite the geographical proximity of Helike to Aigai—both were situated on the Corinthian gulf and the fact that both are mentioned in the *Iliad* as sacred to Poseidon (8.203), the attempts to derive the title Helikônios from Helike rather than from Helikon are linguistically unsound.

5. For Poseidon as an instructor in horsemanship and a tamer of horses, see *Iliad* 23.307; Sophocles *Oedipus Coloneus* 712–15; and Aristophanes *Knights* 551–58.

5–7. Poseidon as savior of ships and sailors may have been replaced by Saint Nikolaos. See notes on hymn 33 to the Dioskouroi. Saint Nikolaos is the patron saint of the Greek navy. Many of the large boats offer to their passengers chapels for prayer to this very popular saint.

23 : To Zeus

In another hymn to Zeus, an impressive one found in Palaikastro, Crete (Bosanquet 1908), we read a similar tribute to his magnificence as in the first line of hymn 23. This extremely short piece is probably a brief prayer. Themis belongs to the generation of the Titans. As the wife of Zeus, Themis is mother of the three Horae (Seasons) and of the three Fates. In the present hymn she is the very image of conjugal trust and conjugal bliss. It is peculiar that Zeus, the highest of the gods, is honored by a hymn only in this unpretentious prelude that he shares with Themis. One wonders whether the father of the gods was felt to be somewhat remote and inaccessible. It is quite interesting that in Greek Orthodoxy, although many benedictions and tropes begin with the phrase "in the name of the Father," it is Jesus, Mary, and the saints who are the favorites of the hymnists. Date and place of composition are unknown. In *Iliad* 14.312–28, Zeus rehearses the names of all the beautiful women he loved and slept with. Although most of the names are Hellenic, originally they may have been the Hellenized names of various divinities that stood for a local version of the earth goddess.

Zeus is invoked as counselor and lawgiver. This is clearly implied by the presence of Themis, whose legal and pacific nature is highlighted by her daughters Eunomia (Good Law), Dikê (Justice), and Eirenê (Peace), concerning whom see Hesiod *Theogony* 901–6. Although, as this Hesiodic passage attests, Themis was Zeus's second wife, here she seems to be more of a *paredros* (an assistant). For Themis in Homer, see *Iliad* 15.87–100 and 20.4–6; *Odyssey* 2.68–9. The claim that Zeus's name survives in Naxos may not be as extravagant as it appears at first. The name of the highest mountain in Naxos is Zas.

24 : To Hestia

Hestia was a virgin goddess, and therefore, she had nothing to do with Aphrodite. There were also certain taboos concerning a man's behavior in her presence. From Hesiod, we learn that after sexual intercourse a man should not appear with exposed genitals before the hearth of his house (*Works and Days* 733–34). See also notes on hymn 29 to Hestia.

Although Hestia was never completely personified, here she is definitely invoked as an anthropomorphic goddess. Originally she was simply the hearth and the fire that burned in the hearth. She was both a familial and a civic deity, since public buildings also contained a hearth on which the well-being of the city depended, much as the well-being of the family depended on the hearth of its dwelling. The hymn does not seem to be earlier than the fifth century BC.

The Roman Vesta is etymologically and semantically related to Hestia. The Roman version developed into a public religious symbol, whereas Hestia was extremely important in domestic cult. She was a symbol of the unity of the family, a sacrosanct symbol. In *Odyssey* 7.153–54, Odysseus sought asylum by sitting next to the fire where he was inviolable. Zeus gave Hestia the privilege of sitting in the middle of the house and of receiving the dripping fat of offerings. When a new colony was founded, fire from the public Hestia of the mother city was transported to it. The light of the resurrection service at the Holy Sepulcher is transported to such Orthodox countries as Greece, Russia, the Ukraine, and so on. Clearly this practice has old roots.

1–2. The reference is to the sacred hearth at Delphoi.

3. Sacrificial oil was frequently poured on sacred stones and on the heads of the divine statues.

4. The occasion seems to be the construction of a new dwelling and not, as some scholars think, of a temple.

5. It was not uncommon to invoke Hestia together with Zeus; in Homer, the hearth is invoked along with Zeus (*Odyssey* 14.158–59), and in time the two deities merged in the concept of Zeus Ephestios ("Zeus of the hearth"). However, our line is still puzzling, because one does not think of gods of the hearth as particularly connected with the grace of song.

25 : To the Muses and Apollon

In the *Iliad,* the Muses sing as Apollon
plays the lyre (1.601–4). The Iliadic scene is
not substantially different from the one in
the *Hymn to Apollon* 3.189–93 (see also the
Hymn to Hermes 4.450–52). The invocation
of Zeus, who is father of both Apollon and
the Muses, is quite natural. Equally natural
is the joint worship of Apollon and the
Muses, because he played the lyre and they
usually sang. Our poet's invocation is most
appropriate, since he presumably is both a
lyre player and a singer. Most commentators
consider this poem some kind of patchwork
from Hesiod *Theogony* 1–104. This hymn
may be as early as the late seventh or, more
probably, the sixth century.

As they are depicted in Hesiod, the Muses seem to represent a classification of the
worthwhile human endeavors. Thus, Kalliope is Muse of Epic Poetry; Kleio, Muse of
History, and so on. They are daughters of
Zeus and Mnemosyne (Memory), which
binds them together and makes each one of
them a contributor to Aletheia (Non-Obliv-
ion). Above all, the Muses were lovely and
inspiring. Both the *Iliad* and the *Odyssey*
begin with an appeal to the Muse that must
be Mnemosyne. In both cases, the singer
needs the help of Mnemosyne to sing such
a long song. It was sometime in the fourth
century that a formal cult and sanctuary
devoted to the Muses were established
below Mount Helikon. However, as early
as Hesiod, Helikon may have been dotted
with small shrines dedicated to the Muses.
Since the Muses were divinities, of course
they were inviolable. They exuded feminine
grace. Statues of the Muses were set up in
the Valley of the Muses. Plato erected a
shrine to the Muses in his Academy (see
Lang 1911). Also, Pausanias, a highly educated traveler of the second half of the second
century AD, bears witness to the existence
of such a shrine (Paus. 1.30, 2).

The eastern slopes of Mount Helikon
face the Valley of the Muses. This lovely
place is located in Thespiai, close to ancient
Askre, Boiotia. The first excavations on the
site of the Valley of the Muses were con-
ducted by the French Archaeological School
between 1880 and 1890. These excavations
were followed by a long period of inactivity
in archaeological research. Archaeologists of
the French Archaeological School worked
on the site again in 2018. Their activities
resumed in 2019 and will hopefully continue
for many summers to come. Most of the
archaeological finds are housed in the new
museum of Thebes.

26 : To Dionysos

In some ways, hymn 26 to Dionysos is a
pictorial triptych: Dionysos being nursed
by the Muses is growing up inside "a
sweet-smelling cave" (6). Hermes as a
child, too, "lived inside a thick-shaded cave"
(*Hymn to Hermes,* 4.6). The divine nurses,
attendants of Dionysos, appear in the
famous ode to Kolonos (Sophocles *Oedipus
Coloneus* 679–81). The baby god steps into
an obviously sacred grove in the company
of his caring nurses, the Nymphs. In Orphic
hymn 46 to Liknites, Dionysos is a "nurs-
ling of the Nymphs and of fair-wreathed
Aphrodite." There are really no similarities
between the Homeric hymns to Dionysos
and the Orphic hymns dedicated to him,
which consist of chains of epithets calcu-
lated to invoke the god. Despite its brevity,
this piece has an honest exuberance such as
one might expect of a song performed at a
Dionysiac festival. The date may be rather
early. See notes to hymns 1 and 7.

Nysa, in line 5, is the name of various
cities in Kylikia, Karia, and Lykia. The composer is using folk etymology to account
for the origin of the name of Dionysos.
Hymn 26 is more powerful, more Dionysiac
than hymns 1 and 7. In hymn 26 the god is
"wreathed with ivy," and when he moves the
vast forest echoes with the din of revelry.

In hymn 7, Dionysos is the god who will
not tolerate any bonds or shackles. His cap-
tors put him in chains, but the chains simply
come off. The god is on a boat, and a vine
appears miraculously while wine is gurgling
all over the place. The god changes shapes.
He becomes a bear and then a lion. In hymn
26, it is the god's connection with nature
and his wild side that are extolled. Here the
god reminds us of Orpheus and his train
of women worshippers. It is possible that
religious ideas about Dionysos came to
the Hellenic world from Northern Europe,

perhaps even from the extreme north where Shamanism was practiced. The process may have been facilitated by the trade of amber (see Athanassakis 2001c).

27 : To Artemis

The hymn is simple and charming. Artemis is depicted as a youthful huntress who comes to Delphoi to lead the Muses and the Graces in the dance. In the earlier stage of the cult of Apollon at Delphoi, Artemis was of little or no importance, but in classical times she was introduced into the cult and even shared some of Apollon's cult epithets (e.g., Delphinia, Pythia). We know that hymns such as this were recited at Delphoi on certain festive occasions, and it is quite possible that our hymn was composed for one of these occasions. Comparison with the long *Hymn to Apollon* shows that the composer of this short *Hymn to Artemis* may have consciously borrowed from the song in honor of the Delphic god.

This hymn may not be earlier than the fifth century BC. In it, mountains and seas shudder as the goddess moves through them. She comes to Delphoi to set up the beautiful dances of the Muses and the Graces. We note here that Alkman's choruses of beautiful and athletic young Spartan women devoted to the cult of Artemis remind us of the aforesaid gathering of the Muses and the Graces at Delphoi. Their song is divine (18). In the promontory of Spathi, Western Crete, we come upon the remains of a temple to Artemis Diktyna. This version of Artemis is an older Cretan goddess later overshadowed and subsumed by Artemis.

At her sacred site in the district of Attica, the goddess becomes Artemis Brauronia. The legends surrounding this cult seem to go back to a bear cult. In this case, Artemis is naturalized and she takes on an epithet that comes from a place name. She is drafted to serve the religious needs of Athens. Close to the well-known Panathenaic stadium, there is the very important temple to Artemis Agrotera, which was built in 448 BC to express gratitude to the goddess for her help in defeating the Persians in the battle of Marathon. This temple is now in danger of being swallowed up by urban development. In *Odyssey* 20.61–90, Penelo-

pe prays to Artemis. We note here that, whereas both in our hymn and elsewhere Artemis is a goddess of the woodlands and mountain peaks, many of her temples are found on littoral space (Spathi, Brauron, Ikaria, Northern Euboea, etc.).

The museum at Brauron is full of statues of little children, mostly little girls but some little boys as well. In some ways, Brauron is the oldest school for little girls. Basic religious ideas concerning the goddess must have been taught here. Perhaps, also, good manners and respect for family values were taught. It was not very long after graduation that the little girls became young brides. Obviously, this is a liminal rite of passage. The procession to Brauron started from the small temple of Artemis in the Acropolis and proceeded to Brauron, thirty-eight kilometers away. Hymn 27 does not mention the important cults of Artemis in Sparta or Ephesos. Missing also from hymn 27 are references to other important cults. The singer concentrates on Artemis, the beautiful archer, the mountain goddess, the sister of Apollon, the daughter of Leto.

In hymn 27 no mention is made of Iphigenia who, according to legend, came to Brauron and became a priestess of Artemis. Relevant to the legend are passages in Euripides *Iphigenia in Tauris*, especially lines 1056–150 and 1456–86. For further details on the cult of Artemis at Brauron, see Nielsen (2009), Lundgreen (2009), Mejer (2009), and Ekroth (2003).

28 : To Athena

Even though there is nothing in the poem betraying the place of its origin, Attica, and especially Athens, would be a good guess, because at no other place was Athena honored as much. In fact, the Panathenaic festival would have been a most fitting occasion for the composition of such a hymn. The date may well be the fifth century.

3. See also hymn 11 to Athena, which is essentially a tribute to Athena as a goddess who protects cities against those who lay sieges intended to sack them.

4. The cult epithet Tritogeneia is of unknown origin and meaning. It may be that this epithet refers to the three classes of people that are associated with Athena's divine ju-

risdiction. Through her birth from the head of Zeus, she is associated with the priestly class that was at the top of hierarchy in Indo-European societies. She is definitely a goddess of warriors and certainly in Athens, as Athena Erganê, she is protectress of the very important class of craftsmen. Such a complex feminine divinity is not associated with the pleasures and intrigues of Aphrodite. For details, see Athanassakis (1989a).

4–12. See the Hesiodic account in *Theogony* 886–900; also Pindar *Olympian Ode* 7.35–44.

Athena is introduced in this hymn as a merciless war goddess. Her armor has the sheen of gold. When she rises before the assembly of the gods and shakes her spear, great Olympos quakes, the earth echoes, and the sea heaves with purple waves. Helios halts his steeds long enough for her to take off her armor. The cosmic proportion of Athena's disarming is measured by the fact that Helios stands still until she completes her act. This reminds us of the beautiful chapters in the Old Testament, when Joshua commands the sun to stand still until the Israelites avenge themselves upon their enemies (Josh. 12–14). At all times, she is a virgin goddess. It was not very difficult for the Christians to replace Athena and put Virgin Mary in her place. In a well-known ninth-century Byzantine hymn, the Theotokos is a leader of armies as well as a defender of her city, Constantinople.

Here are the beginning lines:

> To our commander and ally,
> a song of victory and gratitude,
> the city records for you
> for having redeemed her of suffering,
> Oh mother of God.

This beautiful hymn is sung in Orthodox churches every Friday of the five weeks that precede Easter. It was composed in honor of the Virgin Mary for saving Constantinople from the Avars who had besieged the city in AD 626.

29 : To Hestia

1–6. Hymn 29 makes it clear that Hestia is a very important goddess, especially since every feast and every ritual act begins and ends with her. Hestia is honored with liba-

tions of wine. She is not a goddess to whom animals are sacrificed.

6–14. This joint invocation to Hestia and Hermes may at first appear strange. The reader will readily recall Hermes as messenger of the gods or *psychopompos* (escort of souls) but not as a tutelary household deity. It should be said, however, that this hymn, much like hymn 24, was composed on the occasion of the solemn consecration of a new dwelling. Hermes's phallic statue stood at the entrance to Athenian houses, and in this role the god was not only apotropaic but also surely acted as a protector of the family's fertility. Further, Hermes was a bringer of good luck, and that is exactly what a new home needs. It is a combination of these roles that makes Hermes not a strange but in fact a most natural companion of Hestia for the occasion that we assume as the reason for the poem. There is no clue as to the date or place of composition of the hymn.

Hestia was given the prerogative of a seat at the very center of a house or a hall. She was also given an honorific portion of the beginning and the end of any sacrifice. There is virtually no mythology attached to Hestia, both because she was a virgin goddess and because she was stationary in the dwelling. As a virgin goddess, Hestia presides over the sanctity of every home. As we learn from hymn 5 to Aphrodite, Hestia as well as Artemis and Athena are goddesses that must stay clear of the power of Aphrodite. They are, as it were, gatekeepers to important aspects of city life and domestic safety.

The nomadic Sarakatsanoi, virtually a mountain tribe in Greece until roughly fifty years ago, lived in conical huts, which were circular at the base. Among them, the hearth was placed at the very center of the hut. Most of the vocabulary attached to parts of the hearth and the utensils used to cook in it was also very old (e.g., "pyr," "pyrostia," "gastra," etc.). On Christmas Day or Christmas Eve, as people sit around the fire, a member of the family places branches of holm-oak (Ilex) on the hearth fire. Again, all sorts of noises are produced. They are mini-explosions of gas that shepherds believe promote fertility among the flocks. On the hearth among the Sarakatsanoi, see

Campbell (1964, 150–1). On the Sarakatsanoi in general, see Fermor (2004, 50–63).

30 : To Earth, Mother of All

That there should be echoes from the *Hymn
to Demeter* in this poem is quite natural.
After all, Demeter; Rhea; Kybele; Earth,
Mother of All; and the Mother of the Gods
are nothing less than different versions of
the primeval womb, the archetypal mother,
who has given birth to everything that lives.
Although it is not clear on what occasion
such a poem might have been recited or
sung, it is a true *prooimion*. Its date of composition may fall anywhere within the fifth
and fourth centuries BC.

Gaia was second in order when the
primordial cosmogony took place. She
gave birth to Ouranos and practically to
everything that exists. She then united
sexually with Ouranos, her own enormous
child, and gave birth to the Titans. Hesiod is the authentic source for the myths
surrounding all this. In Homeric hymn 30,
Gaia gives birth to essentially all creation.
She has control over life and death. She also
governs all matters of fertility. At the end of
the hymn, she is saluted as the practically
anthropomorphic wife of Ouranos. However, she never assumed fully human form. At
some point, she gave birth to the monstrous
Typhaòn who rose in rebellion against Zeus
but then was destroyed by him. In Athens,
there was a sanctuary to Gaia Kourotrophos
("nurturer of youths") near the entrance
to the Acropolis. At Eleusis there is a cave
that in very old times was probably a place
of worship for Gaia. Line 6 asserts that Gaia
can give life but also take it. Her undesirable
side has survived in modern Greek dirges,
where she is the black earth that devours
even handsome young men. In Greek
mythology, Delphoi is the navel (*omphalos*)
of the earth, while the area surrounding
Eleusis is the udder of it. Probably, these are
inherited pre-Hellenic elements of Greek
mythology.

The reader should compare the hymn
with Orphic hymn 26. There is, however,
nothing that makes this hymn especially
Orphic. The poet rightly calls the divinity
honored in this hymn "mother of all and
oldest of all" (1–2) because Chaos, which

preceded her, was in essence the Void into
which she was born. Ouranos (Sky), to
whom the generation of all subsequent
Greek gods is to be traced, was her child,
and it was in incestuous union with him
that she gave birth to Kronos (see Hesiod
Theogony 116ff.; 821–57).

31 : To Helios

The reader should compare this hymn with
Orphic hymn 8. Although Helios, the Sun,
was invoked in oaths, Rhodes was the only
place in which he played an important role
in public cult. There is no hint as to the date
and place of composition for either this
hymn or the next one.

In the *Odyssey*, Hyperion is an epithet of
Helios. In hymn 31 there is some confusion.
Hyperion, a Titan, marries Euryphaëssa,
his own sister, and she gives birth to Eos,
Selene, and Helios. It is likely that the original epithets were Helios for Hyperion and
Selene for Euryphaëssa—mighty Sun and
far-shining Moon. The epithets acquired
an independence or simply changed their
syntactic relation to the noun. So, Hyperion
became the father of Helios, and Euryphaëssa became the mother of Selene.

In the *Odyssey*, Helios owns oxen. Odysseus's comrades eat the oxen, and they
are punished for their impious act. These
oxen may have been offered by worshippers
in exchange for protection. This was done
in modern Greece. People offered cattle to
monasteries so they would be protected
from robbers and, formerly, from the Otto-
man authorities. Through partial homonymy, Helios continues to be worshipped on
mountain peaks as Ai-Lias, or the Prophet
Elijah. His feast day is July 20. In my own
birthplace, Astrochori, Arta, a memory of
stag sacrifice survived until recently but
vanished into oblivion when the last man
who knew about it died just before the
end of the twentieth century. There was
a small chapel of Saint Elias on top of the
very rugged peak of Zioura. According to
the oral tradition, a single monk lived there,
and just before he died he left a note that he
could no longer battle the angry elements
of nature. One detail about the stag sacrifice
survives with me to this day. Before the
sacrifice, people would make sure to give

the stag plenty of water so it would not be
thirsty.

1. The customary invocation was to a Muse or
goddess, but Alkman, too, names Kalliope (27 *PMG*, 43 Loeb). It was in later
times, Roman in fact, that the Muses were
differentiated according to their various
functions. Kalliope became traditionally the
Muse of Heroic Epic.

2–7. Euryphaëssa occurs only here. In Hesiod
Theogony 371–74, it is Theia who gives birth
to Helios (Sun), Selene (Moon), and Eos
(Dawn).

8–16. In the hands of later poetasters, the image of Helios on his horses or on a chariot
drawn by horses became virtually hack-
neyed (see Seneca *Apocolocyntosis* 2). The
concept is not Homeric, but common in the
hymns (2.63; 2.88; 4.69; 28.14).

32 : To Selene

Perhaps Selene, the Moon, is perceived
here as long-winged because she, too, needs
wings in order to move on the sky. Hermes
needs wings. Then Iris, the messenger
goddess, is a winged divinity. Selene is associated with Hekate, the "distant one." Se-
lene-Hekate have power over women's lives.
In this hymn, Selene bathes in the streams
of Okeanos. Then she drives her chariot on
the sky to manifest all of her brilliance. Her
beauty did not escape Zeus. He sought her
affection, and a daughter, Pandeia, was born
of the union. Again, Pandeia is simply an
epithet of the moon.

5–13. The splendor that emanates from the
bright moon after her bath in the stream of
ocean is comparable to the splendor of the
victorious horses in Pindar *Olympian Ode*
3.10–15.

13. We read that Selene offers guidance to
people through signs and symbols.

14. This love affair of Zeus with Selene is not
in the catalogue of his amorous accomplishments in Hesiod *Theogony* 886ff.

15. Pandeia's name can be connected with the
adjective "pandios" ("all-luminous") with
reasonable certainty. The daughter is an
extension and an abstraction of the divine
mother. Connection with the Athenian
festival of Pandia has not been definitely
established.

33 : To the Dioskouroi

The Dioskouroi are winged like the archangels Michael and Gabriel. These two
archangels have an honorific position in
the iconography of the Greek Orthodox
Church. Archangel Michael carries a sword.
In modern Greek religious ideology, he has
taken the position of Charon or Hermes. At
the village of Diporo, Mani, there is an impressive church in honor of Saint Stratigos,
the taxiarch and military commander. The
district of Mani has been known for its practice of harsh revenge in cases that involve
violation of honor. The presence of such
a saint in the hagiology of the Orthodox
Church testifies to the practice of accom-
modation and of syncretism between pagan
and Christian ideas. It is possible that the
two physician-saints, the brothers, Kosmas
and Damianos inherited the more benign
aspects of the Dioskouroi.

The cult of the twin Dioskouroi must
have spread out of Sparta, a city with a
tenuous connection to the sea. It was the
usual practice of the early and not-so-early
Church to replace everything "pagan" with
something distinctly Christian. It may not
be accidental that Christians ended up with
two miracle-working saints to whom they
could appeal when they found themselves
in stormy seas. The impressive presence
of the archangels Michael and Gabriel, especially inside Orthodox churches, might be a
lingering memory of the Dioskouroi. Both
are winged and powerful emissaries of God.
The Aśvins of Indic mythology point to
some sort of archetypal entity.

There is a good chance that this hymn
is much older than hymn 17 and that, in
fact, it may antedate the sixth century BC.
Stylistic grounds have led scholars to link it
with hymn 7 to Dionysos and to think that
Theokritos imitated it in *Idyll* 22.

1–3. In the *Iliad*, Kastor, the tamer of horses,
and Polydeukes, the boxer, are not divine.
They are the sons of Tyndareus, mortal
heroes whom Priam, not knowing that
they are dead and buried in Lakedaemon,
expects to see among the other heroes in
Troy (*Iliad* 3.236–45). In the *Odyssey*, this
same tradition is accepted, but it is added,
"Life-giving earth holds them alive and

honored by Zeus even below the earth" (*Odyssey* 11.301–4). The tradition that makes Zeus the father of Kastor and Polydeukes is therefore post-Homeric, and its earliest occurrence must be Hesiod's *Ehoiai* (66 Loeb). The patronymic Tyndaridai refers to their putative father, and it was used both in literature and cult. There is no trace here of Leda's seduction by Zeus in the form of a swan. According to the older tradition, only Helen was born of that peculiar union (Euripides *Helena* 16–22). It was obviously the Alexandrian mythographers who had the divine twins hatched out of the swan's egg. In any case, Zeus granted them the status of heroes who came with wealth and eternal life on the islands of the blessed (Hesiod *Works and Days* 156–173).

5. Lakonia was the center from which the worship of the Dioskouroi spread to other parts of Greece.

6–19. The Dioskouroi, saviors of men who are in danger of losing their lives in stormy seas, come to their help. Winged as they are, they move very swiftly to still the perilous winds. Their ability to control thunderstorms is clearly something they have inherited from their father. After all, Zeus is the god of thunder and lightning. At some point, Saint Nikolas, archbishop of Myra in Kilikia, and Saint Elmo of Formia, South Italy, displaced the Dioskouroi as protectors of seamen and assumed this function. Apropos of this, it is possible that in the Eastern Orthodox Church at least, the twin Dioskouroi survived also as the archangels Michael and Gabriel. It is quite possible that it was their role in the Argonautic saga that secured the heroic twins their wonder-working role as saviors of imperiled sailors. Their epiphany usually took the form of the twin lights of St. Elmo's fire. This identification eventually led to astral connections, especially with the constellation of the Gemini. Interesting speculations have been made about the relationship of Kastor and Polydeukes to the Aśvin, the divine horseriding twins of Sanskrit mythology, but nothing conclusive has been proven.

To Guest-Friends

Codex *M* does not contain this piece, which is included in manuscripts of the *X* family and in manuscripts *C* and *D*. The version of the hymn corpus and that of the *Vita Herodotea* show great textual divergence.

It is incorrect to translate the title as *To Strangers,* especially in view of the first line of the poem, where the word "xenia" ("gifts of guestfriendship") clearly defines the meaning of the title. The fact that the poem is in the *Vita Herodotea* (approximately AD 200) does not indicate that it was transferred from it to the corpus of the hymns. Its date is unknown, and it seems to be Aeolic, or at least Chian, in origin. The piece has been taken as an *envoi* by the poet of the hymns to the inhabitants of Aeolic Kymê, by the river Hermos. Saidene is not such a well-known city. The same is not true of Hermos, the river that in the *Iliad* is the son of Zeus (20.392). Greek culture had a cheerful view of entertaining guests. However, the idea was not that the world is full of friends but rather that the world was full of potential friends.

SELECT BIBLIOGRAPHY

Aign, B. 1963. *Die Geschichte der Musikinstrumente des Ägäischen Raumes bis um 700 vor Christus: ein Beitrag zur Vor- und Frühgeschichte der griechischen Musik.* Germany: Frankfurt am Main. Universität.

Alderink, L. J. 1982. "Mythological and Cosmological Structure in the Homeric Hymn to Demeter." *Numen* 29, no. 1: 1–16.

Alexiou, M. 2002. *The Ritual Lament in Greek Tradition.* 2nd ed. Oxford: Rowman & Littlefield.

Allen, T. W. 1983. *Homeri Opera.* Vol. 5. Oxford: Oxford University Press.

Allen, T. W., W. R. Halliday, and E. E. Sikes. 1936. *The Homeric Hymns.* 2nd ed. Oxford: Clarendon Press (London: Milford).

Arthur, M. 1977. "Politics and Pomegranates: An Interpretation of the Homeric *Hymn to Demeter.*" *Arethusa* 10, no. 1: 7–47.

Athanassakis, A. N. 1976. "Music and Ritual in Primitive Eleusis." *Platon* 28: 86–105.

———. 1988. "Gods, Heroes, and Saints against the Dragon." *The Ancient World* 17: 41–63.

———. 1989a. "The Birth of Athena Tritogeneia." *Hellenica* 40, no 1: 7–21.

———. 1989b. "From the Phallic Cairn to Shepherd God and Divine Herald." *Eranos* 87: 33–49.

———. 2001a. "Europe: Early Geographic and Mythic Identity." *Dodoni* 22: 283–303.

———. 2001b. "Proteus, the Old Man of the Sea: Homeric Merman or Shaman? La mythologies et L'Odysee: Homage a Gabriel Germain." *Special Issue of Gaia (Grenoble)* 5: 45–56.

———. 2001c. Shamanism and Amber in Greece: The Northern Connection. In *Shamanhood: Symbolism and Epic,* edited by J. Pentikäinen, 203–20. Budapest: Akadémiai Kiadó.

———. 2004a. *Hesiod: Theogony, Works and Days, Shield.* Baltimore and London: Johns Hopkins University Press.

———. 2004b. *The Homeric Hymns.* 2nd ed. Baltimore and London: Johns Hopkins University Press.

———. 2006. "Greek Bear Mythology." In *On the Footsteps of the Bear,* edited by Clive Tolley, 84–93. Pori, Finland: University of Turku and Satakunta Museum.

———. 2007. "Catalogs of Names in the *Iliad* and the *Odyssey.*" *Proceedings of the International Congress of Odyssean Studies* 10: 261–267.

Athanassakis, A. N., and B. M. Wolkow. 2013. *The Orphic Hymns.* Baltimore: Johns Hopkins University Press.

Bergren, A.L.T. 1989. "The Homeric Hymn to Aphrodite: Tradition and Rhetoric, Praise and Blame." *Classical Antiquity* 8, no. 1: 1–41.

Bickerman, E. J. 1976. "Love Story in the Homeric Hymn to Aphrodite." *Athenaeum* 54: 229–54.

Boedeker, D. D. 1974. *Aphrodite's Entry into Greek Epic.* Leiden, Neth.: Brill.

Bosanquet, R. C. 1908. "The Palaikastro Hymn of the Kouretes." *The Annual of the British School at Athens* 15: 339–56.

Brown, N. O. 1947. *Hermes the Thief.* Madison: University of Wisconsin Press.

Burkert, W. 1985. *Greek Religion.* Cambridge, MA: Basil Blackwell and Harvard University Press.

Bush, D. 1968. *Pagan Myth and Christian Tradition in English Poetry.* Philadelphia: American Philosophical Society.

Campbell, J. K. 1964. *Honour, Family, and Patronage: A Study of Institutions and Moral Values in a Greek Mountain Community.* New York: Oxford University Press.

Clay, J. S. 1981–82. "Immortal and Ageless Forever." *Classical Journal* 77, no. 2: 112–17.

———. 1983. *The Wrath of Athena.* Princeton, NJ: Princeton University Press.

———. 1987. "Hermes' Dais by the Alpheus: *Hymn to Hermes,* 105–141." *Métis* 2: 221–34.

————. 1989. *The Politics of Olympus.* Princeton, NJ: Princeton University Press.

————. 1997. "The Homeric Hymns." In *A New Companion to Homer,* edited by I. Morris and B. Powell, 489–507. Leiden, Neth., and New York: Brill.

Clinton, K. 1993. "The Sanctuary of Demeter and Kore at Eleusis." In *Greek Sanctuaries: New Approaches,* edited by N. Marinatos and R. Hägg, 110–24. London and New York: Routledge.

Dowden, K. 1989. *Death and the Maiden: Girls' Initiation Rites in Greek Mythology.* London and New York: Routledge.

Ekroth, G. 2003. "Inventing Iphigenia? On Euripides and the Cultic Construction of Brauron." *Kernos* 16: 59–118.

Farnell, L. R. 1896–1909. *The Cults of the Greek States.* 5 vols. Oxford: Clarendon.

Fermor, P. L. 2004. *Roumeli: Travels in Northern Greece.* London: John Murray.

Flach, I., ed. 1883. *Biographi Graeci qui ab Hesychio pendent.* Berlin: S. Calvary Eiusque Socius.

Foley, H. P. 1994. *The Homeric Hymn to Demeter.* Princeton, NJ: Princeton University Press.

Fontenrose, J. E. 1959. *Python: A Study of Delphic Myth and Its Origins.* Berkeley: University of California Press.

————. 1978. *The Delphic Oracle.* Berkeley: University of California Press.

Foote, P. G., and D. M. Wilson. 1973 (1970). *The Viking Achievement: The Society and Culture of Early Medieval Scandinavia.* London: Sidgwick & Jackson.

Frazer, J. G. 1917–19. *The Golden Bough.* London: Macmillan.

————. 1921. *Apollodorus: The Library.* 2 vols. London and Cambridge, MA: Harvard University Press.

————. 1967 (1921). "Putting Children on the Fire." In *Apollodorus: The Library,* vol. 2, 311–17. London and Cambridge, MA: Harvard University Press.

Friedrich, P. 1978. *The Meaning of Aphrodite.* Chicago: University of Chicago Press.

Gantz, T. 1993. *Early Greek Myth: A Guide to Literary and Artistic Sources.* Vol. 1. Baltimore and London: Johns Hopkins University Press.

Giacomelli, A. 1980. "Aphrodite and After." *Phoenix* 34, no. 1: 1–19.

Giannakis, G. K. 1998. "Το ποιητικό Μοτίβο 'Γάμος-Θάνατος' στην Αρχαία Ελληνική και την Ινδοευρωπαϊκή" ["The poetic motif 'marriage-death' in Ancient Greek and Indo-European"]. *Dodoni* 27: 94–113.

Graf, F., and S. I. Johnston. 2013. *Ritual Texts for the Afterlife.* London: Routledge.

Harrison, J. E. 1991 (1903). *Prolegomena to the Study of Greek Religion.* Princeton, NJ: Princeton University Press.

Herzfeld, M. 1985. *The Poetics of Manhood.* Princeton, NJ: Princeton University Press.

Hornblower, S., A. Spawforth, and E. Eidinow, eds. 2012. *The Oxford Classical Dictionary.* 4th ed. Oxford: Oxford University Press.

Hunter, R. 2005. *The Hesiodic Catalogue of Women: Constructions and Reconstructions.* Cambridge: Cambridge University Press.

James, A. W. 1975. "Dionysus and the Tyrrhenic Pirates." *Antichthon* 9: 17–34.

Jameson, M. 1969. "The Mysteries of Eleusis." *Bulletin of the Philadelphia Association for Psychoanalysis* 19, no. 3: 114–32.

Janko, R. 1981. "The Structure of the Homeric Hymns: A Study in Genre." *Hermes* 109: 9–24.

————. 1982. *Homer, Hesiod and the Hymns: Diachronic Development in Epic Diction.* Cambridge: Cambridge University Press.

Jung, C. G., ed. 1964. *Man and His Symbols.* New York: Doubleday.

————. 1967. "The Psychological Aspects of the Kore." In *Essays on a Science of Mythology: The Myth of the Divine Child,* by C. G. Jung and K. Kerényi, 156–77. Princeton, NJ: Princeton University Press.

Kaimio, M. 1974. "Music in the Homeric Hymn to Hermes." *Arctos* 8: 29–42.

Kazantzakis, N. 1985. *The Odyssey: A Modern Sequel.* Translated by K. Friar. New York: Simon and Schuster.

Kerényi, K. 1967. *Eleusis: The Archetypical Image of Mother and Daughter.* Translated by R. Manheim. Princeton, NJ: Princeton University Press.

Kern, O. 1922. *Orphicorum Fragmenta*. Berlin: Apud Weidmannos.

King, H. 1986. "Tithonos and the Tettix." *Arethusa* 19, no. 1: 15–32.

Kirk, G. S. 1970. *Myth: Its Meaning and Functions in Ancient and Other Cultures*. Berkeley: University of California Press.

Lang, P. 1911. *De Speusippi academici scriptis accedunt fragmenta*. Bonnae: Typis C. Georgi Typographi Academici

Larson, J. 1995. "The Corycian Nymphs and the Bee Maidens of the Homeric *Hymn to Hermes*." *Greek, Roman and Byzantine Studies* 36: 341–57.

Lawler, L. B. 1978. *The Dance in Ancient Greece*. Middletown: Wesleyan University Press.

Lincoln, B. 1979. "The Rape of Persephone: A Greek Scenario of Women's Initiation." *Harvard Theological Review* 72, no. 3: 223–35.

Lundgreen, B. 2009. "Boys at Brauron." *Acta Hyperborea* 12: 117–26.

Mejer, J. 2009. "Artemis in Athens." *Acta Hyperborea* 12: 61–78.

Miller, A. M. "The 'Address to the Delian Maidens' in the Homeric *Hymn to Apollo*: Epilogue or Transition?" *Transactions of the American Philological Association* 109 (1979): 173–86.

Motsios, G. 2000. *Το ελληνικό Μοιρολόγι. Τόμος Β* [The Greek lament. Vol. 2]. Athens: Kodikas.

———. 2007–2009. *Δωδώνη: Ανέκδοτα μοιρολόγια της Περιοχής Γρεβενών* [Dodoni: unpublished laments from the district of Grevena]. Ioannina: Classics Department.

Mylonas, G. 1942. *The Hymn to Demeter and Her Sanctuary at Eleusis*. St. Louis, MO: Washington University Studies and Language and Literature Studies.

———. 1972 (1961). *Eleusis and the Eleusinian Mysteries*. Princeton, NJ: Princeton University Press.

Nagy, G. 1986. "Ancient Greek Epic and Praise Poetry: Some Typological Considerations." In *Oral Tradition: Interpretation in Context*, edited by J. M. Foley, 89–102. Columbia: University of Missouri Press.

———. 1990. *Greek Mythology and Poetics*. Ithaca, NY: Cornell University Press.

———. 1996. *Homeric Questions*. Austin: University of Texas Press.

Neumann, E. 1974 (1963). *The Great Mother: An Analysis of the Archetype*. Translated by R. Manheim. Princeton, NJ: Princeton University Press.

Nielsen, I. 2009. "The Sanctuary of Artemis Brauronia: Can Architecture and Iconography Help to Locate the Settings of the Rituals?" *Acta Hyperborea* 12: 83–116.

Nilsson, M. P. 1921. *Die Anfänge der Göttin Athene*. Copenhagen: Bianco Lunos

———. 1963. *The Mycenaean Origin of Greek Mythology*. New York: W. W. Norton (Berkeley, 1932, Sather Lectures 8).

Nimas, T. A. 1983. *Δημοτικά Τραγούδια της Θεσσαλίας* [Folk songs of Thessaly]. 2 vols. Thessaloniki: Kyriakidis.

Notopoulos, J. A. 1962. "The Homeric Hymns as Oral Poetry: A Study of the Post-Homeric Oral Tradition." *American Journal of Philology* 83, no. 4: 337–68.

Ormand, K. 2014. *The Hesiodic Catalogue of Women and Archaic Greece*. Cambridge: Cambridge University Press.

Parker, R. 1991. "The *Hymn to Demeter* and the Homeric Hymns." *Greece and Rome* 38, no. 1: 1–17.

Parry, H. 1986. "The *Homeric Hymn to Aphrodite*: Erotic 'Ananke.'" *Phoenix* 40, no. 3: 253–64.

Politis, N. G. 1978. *Εκλογαί από τα Τραγούδια του Ελληνικού Λαού* [Selections from the songs of the Greek people]. Athens: E. G. Vagionaki, 205–28.

Psychogiou, E. 2008. *"Μαυρηγη" και Ελένη. Τελετουργίες Θανάτου και Αναγέννησης* ["Blackearth" and Eleni: Rituals of death and rebirth]. Athens: Akadimia Athinon.

Radin, P. 1956. *The Trickster: A Study in American Indian Mythology*. With commentaries by K. Kerényi and C. G. Jung. London: Routledge and Kegan Paul.

Richardson, N. J. 1974. *The Homeric Hymn to Demeter*. Oxford: Clarendon.

Rose, H. J. 1924. "Anchises and Aphrodite." *Classical Quarterly* 18, no. 1: 11–16.

Sachs, C. 1940. *The History of Musical Instruments*. New York: W. W. Norton.

Saunier, G. 1999. *Ελληνικά Δημοτικά Τραγούδια: Τα Μοιρολόγια* [Greek folk Songs: Dirges]. Athens: Nefeli.

Schachter, A. 1976. "Homeric *Hymn to Apollo,* lines 231–238 (The Onchestus Episode): Another Interpretation." *Bulletin of the Institute of Classical Studies of the University of London* 23, no. 1: 102–14.

Scheinberg, S. 1979. "The Bee Maidens of the Homeric *Hymn to Hermes.*" *Harvard Studies in Classical Philology* 83: 1–28.

Shelmerdine, S. C. 1984. "Hermes and the Tortoise: A Prelude to Cult." *Greek, Roman and Byzantine Studies* 25: 201–7.

———. 1995. *The Homeric Hymns.* Newburyport, MA: Focus / R. Pullins.

Slater, P. E. 1992 (1968). *The Glory of Hera: Greek Mythology and the Greek Family.* Princeton, NJ: Princeton University Press.

Snell, B., and H. Maehler. 1987. *Pindari Carmina cum Fragmentis.* Leipzig, Ger.: Teubner.

Sourvinou-Inwood, C. 1988. *Studies in Girls' Transitions.* Athens: Kardamitsa.

———. 1991. *Reading Greek Culture: Texts and Images, Rituals and Myths.* Oxford: Clarendon.

Sowa, C. A. *Traditional Themes and the Homeric Hymns.* Chicago: Bolchazy Carducci, 1984.

Stephanus Byzantinus. 1849. *Ethnica.* Edited by August Meineke. Berlin: Reimer.

Stillwell, R., W. L. MacDonald, and M. H. McAllister, eds. 1976. *The Princeton Encyclopedia of Classical Sites.* Princeton, NJ: Princeton University Press.

Szepes, E. 1980. "Humour of the *Homeric Hermes Hymn.*" *Homonoia* 2: 5–56.

Vermeule, E. 1979. *Aspects of Death in Early Greek Art and Poetry.* Berkeley: University of California Press.

Vernant, J.-P. 1979. *Myth and Society in Ancient Greece.* Originally published in Paris, 1974. Atlantic Highlands, NJ: Prometheus Books.

———. 2006. *Myth and Thought among the Greeks.* Translated by J. Lloyd and J. Fort. New York: Urzone.

Walcot, P. 1991. "The Homeric *Hymn to Aphrodite:* A Literary Appraisal." *Greece and Rome* 38, no. 2: 137–55.

Walton, F. R. 1952. "Athens, Eleusis, and the Homeric *Hymn to Demeter.*" *Harvard Theological Review* 45, no. 2: 105–14.

Wasson, G. R., A. Hoffmann, and C. A. P. Ruck. 1978. *The Road to Eleusis: Unveiling the Secret of the Mysteries.* New York and London: Harcourt.

West, M. L. 1975. "Cynaethus' Hymn to Apollo." *Classical Quarterly* 25, no. 2: 161–70.

Woolger, J. B., and R. J. Woolger. 1989. *The Goddess Within: A Guide to the Eternal Myths That Shape Women's Lives.* New York: Fawcett Columbine.

INDEX